When I wanted the world ~~to know my story, the person I chose was~~ Cec Murphey! The Walt Disney Company ~~optioned the rights~~ to my story immediately after publishing my first book, and Cec cowrote my second book with me as well. If you want to make an impact on people and challenge the status quo in writing, you better be sure to use the Murphey Method!

    -Salome Thomas-EL: Award-winning Educator, Author of *I Choose to Stay* and *The Immortality of Influence*

Whether you're thinking about venturing into the field, you're an author considering using a ghostwriter, or you just need some good advice on how to positively live your life, *Ghostwriting: The Murphey Method,* is for you. It is full of valuable perception and information based on his personal experiences as well as the basic "how to" needed to understand the pros and cons of ghostwriting. I encourage you to take advantage of Cec's vast knowledge and experience.

    -Eva Piper: Speaker and Author (with Cecil Murphey) of *A Walk Through the Dark: How My Husband's 90 Minutes in Heaven Deepened My Faith for a Lifetime*

I have experienced first-hand the magic of Cec navigating my soul and bringing my story to life. He masterfully has an uncanny ability to take a story and pull focus and give perspective. He knows how to take the most bankrupt soul and give significance and meaning. *Ghostwriting: The Murphey Method* is compelling, rare in our time, and a must for all aspiring students and artisans of the written word.

    -Stan Cottrell: Global Goodwill Ambassador, World Distance Runner, 2017 Nobel Peace Prize Nominee, Inspirational Speaker and Author

Buy this book and read it. Now. You'll be reading the advice of a master of ghostwriting. Cec Murphey has been a gift to our generation, and through each chapter of this book he leaves footsteps of his legacy to those who would follow.

    -Peter Lundell: Author, Speaker, Collaborator/Ghostwriter

Cec Murphey promised God and himself never to stop learning. He has kept his promise. In *Ghostwriting: The Murphey Method*, he generously shares what he wished someone had taught him when he began ghostwriting in 1982, as well as all he has since learned and continues to learn. This is a must-read book for ghostwriters, collaborators, or anyone interested in using their gift with words to express the words in the heart of someone else. Practical, insightful, honest—I highly recommend this book.

-Marlene Bagnull, Litt D: Director, Colorado Christian Writers Conference and Greater Philly Christian Writers Conference

I know of no one better qualified to write a book on ghostwriting than Cec Murphey. He has ghosted or coauthored scores of titles, including a number of best-sellers. If I needed a capable collaborator for a project my company hopes to publish, I would check with Cec first.

In crisp, clear prose that is his hallmark, Cec breaks down the massive undertaking that is collaborative writing into easily digested chunks of information, putting ghostwriting within the reach of many skilled writers. Might ghostwriting be right for you? In Cec's words, "Why not?" If you've ever considered helping others write what they can't write themselves, you must read this book!

-Steve T. Barclift: Managing Editor, Kregel Publications

After reading *Ghostwrting: The Murphey Method*, I can recall the step-by-step process and professional way Cec helped me construct my story, never putting words into my mouth, and making sense out of my rambling without changing my emotion or way of viewing what had happened to me. Even though it was hard work reliving my past, Cecil kept me at a comfort level that I actually enjoyed. I witnessed my story come to life right before my eyes. Because of this first-hand experience, I can see how a writer, seasoned or just beginning their craft, could benefit from reading this book.

-John Turnipseed: Executive Vice President of Urban Ventures, Author of *BloodLine: The True Story of John Turnipseed*

Based on his extensive experience and practical approach, Cec Murphey has written the definitive guidebook on ghostwriting. His transparency and examples provide a realistic assessment of what is involved; and his specific guidelines on how to do it benefit both writers who are exploring this option and those who have already started in this field.

-Lin Johnson: Director, Write-to-Publish Conference

When it comes to writing, Cec Murphey is the ultimate pro. His several books on the topic have helped many authors improve their craft, including me. Now with his newest, *Ghostwriting: The Murphey Method,* Cec gives us an inside look at how he's been able to write best-sellers based on the experiences of men and women who needed help telling their story. Highly recommended!

-Nick Harrison: Agent with WordServe Literary, Author of *Magnificent Prayer* and *Power in the Promises*

In this book, my friend and coauthor captures the practical steps as well as the essential heart behind being a successful ghostwriter. As a ghostwriter, Cec brilliantly brings to life messages trapped in the mind of non-writers, and this book shows you how you can do it too!

-Barry H. Spencer: America's No Regrets Entrepreneur, Author of *The Secret of Wealth With No Regrets*

Whenever I think of Cec Murphey and ghostwriting or collaborative writing, the song "Nobody Does it Better" goes through my mind. A lifetime of expertise is in this book. Every writer can benefit from the lessons found on these pages.

-Steve Laube, President, The Steve Laube Agency and President, The Christian Writers Institute

GHOSTWRITING

THE MURPHEY METHOD

CECIL MURPHEY

CHRISTIAN
WRITERS
INSTITUTE

GHOSTWRITING: THE MURPHEY METHOD by Cecil Murphey
Published by The Christian Writers Institute
24 W. Camelback Rd. A-635
Phoenix, AZ 85013
www.christianwritersinstitute.com

ISBN (paper): 978-1-621840-82-4

Ghostwriting: The Murphey Method
Copyright © 2017 by Cecil Murphey

Published in association with The Knight Agency, Inc., 570 East Avenue, Madison, GA 30650. (www.theknightagency.com)

Cover design by Five J's Design (www.fivejsdesign.com)

Printed in the United States of America

TABLE OF CONTENTS

Introduction

My Ghostwriting
Career Begins

"You know how to get into the heads of other people," Victor Oliver, the editorial director of Fleming H. Revell, said to me.[1] He paused before adding, "I'd like you to ghostwrite a book for us."

His words shocked me, but because he believed in me, I said yes. Then I asked a question: "How do I do it?"

"You'll figure it out." Those may not have been his exact words, but that was certainly the meaning.

Although we spoke for perhaps forty-five minutes, I don't recall that he gave me any specific instructions on how to ghostwrite. That happened in 1982, long before the Internet. I figured it out, worked with the *author*, completed writing the manuscript, and mailed it in to the publishing house. To my surprise, the editors liked my writing.

Victor gave me a second assignment. Others followed. In fact, I wrote thirty-five books for Revell before the editorial director left.

---

1 Revell is now part of the Baker Publishing Group.

That began my career of writing for other people, often celebrities. And in those days, we were truly ghostwriters—we left no evidence in the book that anyone but the *author* had written the book.

Perhaps it sounds as if learning to ghostwrite a book was easy; it wasn't. I found it frustrating and difficult trying to capture what the author intended. Previously I had published nine books of my own, mostly with small presses, and knew nothing about trying to sound like someone else.

Ghostwriting for me was, and remains, a fun but torturous learning experience. Even after I turned in my first project, I still wasn't sure what I was doing. But I *was* learning.

What you'll read in this book truly is the Murphey method—which is the title suggested by Shawn Kuhn, who prompted me to write on this topic. He urged me to help other writers figure out how to write like someone other than themselves. That's what I've tried to do.

Over the past dozen years, I've trained, mentored, or guided about a dozen others in learning to ghostwrite. As I've worked with them, I've continued to learn and improve.

I am a growing writer;
I've promised God and myself never to stop learning.

That might be a good promise for you to make.

1

ME? A GHOSTWRITER?

So you think you'd like to become a ghostwriter.

Or perhaps explore the possibility.

Why not?

Even though it may sound easy, ghostwriting isn't the kind of writing every scribe can do successfully. It requires specific skills and particular personality traits to be good at the task.

Maybe you're one of those who could succeed.

Why not?

I've had a long career of being a professional ghostwriter. Since 1984, I've made a living from this form of publishing, and I'm willing to share what I know.

When I started, we had no Internet. And as far as I could discover, no books existed on ghostwriting (and few publishers openly admitted that celebrities didn't write their own books.) ✓ Yates Therefore, I'm willing to tell you what I wish someone had taught me.

• • •

I began my collaborating in the old typewriter days, and many things have changed over the years. Part of the reason

I've been successful is that I've changed with the times. And it's more than moving from the typewriter to the computer.

Writing styles have changed. For example, you may have noticed the short paragraphs in this book. Thirty years ago, the single biggest battle I had with editors was that they wanted to combine paragraphs and make some of them twelve or fourteen lines in print. I had no editorial rights, and I had to accept whatever the editors decreed.

Although it didn't say so in most of our contracts, the understood policy was that we didn't tell anyone in the public—ever—that we wrote for the famous and the notorious. That's no longer true, and ghostwriters are increasingly known within the publishing industry.

Another factor is that I wrote books for others and did nothing to promote them except tell family members and a few friends about them or buy extra copies to give away. In two of my early royalty contracts, I agreed *not* to promote or publicize the books. With ghostwriters that hasn't changed much—the *authors* have the burden of promoting their books. We *writers* have the burden of promoting our services.

But after I moved into collaboration,[2] my role changed, and I had editorial rights. That is, my byline appeared on the cover, and I began a limited amount of work as part of the promotion team. Increasingly publishers are not only allowing, but encouraging us writers to promote the books we write for others. I suppose anything that produces book sales is acceptable.

• • •

---

2   See chapter 2, where I explain the difference between ghostwriting and collaboration.

Most people assume that ghostwriting refers only to non-fiction, but that's not accurate. In the 1990s, I ghosted two end-time novels for Dr. Michael Youssef.

In the early 1980s, when Christian fiction was hardly known or accepted, I also wrote a series of romantic-suspense novels for what I call a prissy publishing house. The editor believed that conservative people, especially church members, would think fiction written by a man was vulgar. Consequently, she insisted I invent three female pseudonyms for my novels. (The novels weren't very good, so I'm glad people don't associate me with them.)

I know of several novelists who use ghostwriters. It's common knowledge that the more recent novels by V. C. Andrews are ghosted. They'd better be; she died in 1986. Publishers have sometimes tried claiming that an author had completed a series of books, and they published them posthumously. Do you suppose the public really believes that?

When I was a kid, I thought that was true of Zane Grey. He died in 1939, and his publisher, Harper and Row, claimed they had a stockpile of unpublished manuscripts by the late author and continued to publish under his name until 1963. If true, Grey must have been a prolific author to have so many novels left after he departed this life.

In recent years ghostwriters have been producing novels in the style of famous authors—those whose books hit the best-seller list. Many publishers want their top sellers to produce a book a year; not all writers can spit them out that quickly. Hence, there's an excellent opportunity for ghostwriters.

It's well known that the demand for the late Tom Clancy's action novels exceeded his ability to write new books late in his career; consequently, the publisher hired people to write techno-thrillers in the Clancy style. The books did quite well.

The late President John F. Kennedy won the Pulitzer Prize for his *Profiles of Courage*. Even though he claimed he wrote it, it's commonly accepted that his friend and speechwriter, Ted Sorenson, was the man behind the book.

The point of the preceding section is to point out why the term *ghostwriter* has been around for centuries. Publishers considered ghostwriting an honorable profession. Within the past quarter century, the window has been opened to show that not only is the profession honorable, but that ghosts are real people with services to offer others.

TAKEAWAYS

- Ghostwriting is an honorable profession and has been around for centuries.
- Ghostwriting could become your profession.

2

GHOSTWRITER, COLLABORATOR, OR BOOK DOCTOR?

I want to define a few terms. The first is *ghostwriter*. Publishing has a long tradition of using ghostwriters to write books, speeches, articles, and pamphlets for others. In most contracts, those who do the work are referred to as *writers* and those for whom they write as *authors*.

Ghostwriting, however, means the writers remain invisible, as the term implies. Although many are well paid, a ghost receives no credit for the manuscript. However, the writers may list their credits on the vita page of book proposals.

Kind and conscientious authors credit the writers, sometimes laughably. I once received thanks "for writing the first draft of this book." Dennis Hensley told me that he once received thanks for *proofreading* the manuscript. A ghostwriter for women's fiction received thanks for *inspiring* the author.

This naturally raises a question: When, if ever, can writers insert themselves or their stories into a book? Although I've never read an answer, I've discussed this issue several times with my ghostwriting friends.

Some writers, knowing they won't receive credit, have done things like putting little comments within the manuscript such as, "As my good friend, XXX, says," and then quoting themselves, the writers. I consider those legitimate intrusions.

My first ghostwritten project was the autobiography of a then-famous country-and-western singer. Readers won't find a hint of anyone else writing the book, but if they ever listened to the singer ramble between songs, they'd know he couldn't possibly have written his own autobiography. He's a talented singer; he's not a writer.

As explained to me in 1982, when I ghosted that first book, readers wanted to believe that the celebrities themselves typed every word. For the next eight years, I wrote books purportedly by famous individuals, and none of them carried my byline. As well as I can remember, only one of them credited my help.

Stan Cottrell, for whom I wrote *No Mountain Too High* (my second ghostwritten project), insisted on giving me credit. On a page by itself, immediately following the table of contents, he inserted:

Special Thanks
To Cecil B. ("Cec") Murphey,
who helped write this book,
who has learned to understand me, and who,
most of all, has become my friend.

Those were Stan's own words, and I hadn't asked for any recognition. And I'm grateful.

• • •

The second term is *collaborator.* In 1990, I became a collaborator, because it was the first time my name appeared on the cover and the title page along with the author. The book was *Gifted Hands: The Ben Carson Story.*

Dr. Carson's name stood out in large, bold letters, and below that, in one-fourth the size, were three words: "with Cecil Murphey." (I'm not complaining about my name being in smaller type; I'm grateful it was there.) I think it also reminded perceptive readers that this was a cooperative venture.

That book, published jointly by Review & Herald and Zondervan, was released in hardcover, soft cover, and mass paper, and has never been out of print. It's currently in its twenty-fifth year. Much of the success of my career stemmed from the fact that my editor at Review & Herald, Penny Wheeler, along with her committee, insisted on my name being there.

I'm not claiming to be the first ghostwriter ever named, but I wasn't aware of any publishers using the word *with* before that. Regardless of when we first received credit, the term *collaborator* now usually means that the writer's name appears on the cover. The writing is the same with or without credit.

Because I now write books with my name as a shared byline, I have little problems inserting any comments from me. I write, "My cowriter, Cecil Murphey, says . . ." I usually insert my name only once or twice in the entire book. After that it's simply, "My cowriter tells about . . ." I've put the cowriter remarks in many books, and no one has objected.

The publisher of one of my books written in the early '90s (and long out of print) refused to put my name on the cover, but did put it on the title page (and misspelled my surname as *Murphy*). Their reasoning was that if prospective buyers saw my name on the cover, they wouldn't buy it.

"And opening to the title page won't change that?" I asked.

"Oh, they won't even notice," the editor said.

• • •

I need to explain that all this is a little confusing to some people because of the use of another word before the writer's name. That's the word *and*. When two or more authors openly cooperate on a book, they share the byline.

For instance, when I was a teen, I read books by Charles Nordhoff and James Norman Hall such as *Mutiny on the Bounty* and *Pitcairn's Island*. Although Nordhoff wrote a number of books on his own, he shared authorship with Hall on several projects.

When I wrote *90 Minutes in Heaven* for Don Piper, it was natural that I have *with* as part of my byline. When I wrote the proposal, I wrote the title and below it, in smaller letters, I typed *with Cecil Murphey*. The material was Don's, and everything came from his perspective. However, I did three more books with Don, and the byline for those three was *by Don Piper and Cecil Murphey*. That made me his cowriter.

That simple word *and* announces to anyone who understands publishing that I contributed some of the content of the book. In addition, I'm grateful to Don Piper, who understood and was generous in giving me freedom to add material.

Even now Don's newsletters sometimes refer to my books and to me. Not many authors are that considerate and kind.

• • •

Another term, now usually reserved for articles, is *as told to*, which I don't see often. A few years ago, a mining tragedy occurred in Appalachia, and the published book about it came from the perspective of nine miners. In that case, the publisher listed their names and below that used "as told to" followed by the writer. That made sense to me.

• • •

Sometimes we ghostwriters have choices about getting credit for writing a book. It's well-known in publishing that a famous best-selling Texas pastor didn't write one word of his books, and the writer received no credit. However, as the watercooler talk goes, the publisher gave the unnamed scribe a choice. That is, by not using his name, the writer received a larger flat fee for his efforts. (I've heard the additional offer was as low as $15,000 and as high as $40,000.)

In this book, I'll use ghostwriter and collaborator interchangeably, although you know the difference.

• • •

The third term is *book doctor*. What's a book doctor? Before I go into detail, what some people call ghostwriting is really book doctoring. Here's the difference. Ghostwriting means the writer starts with nothing. The author may have a full or partial manuscript, but in the instances where that's been the case, I used the manuscript only for reference. Not out of grandiosity or pride, but it's extremely difficult for people to tell about themselves in print. They tend to ignore the most dramatic points (or don't know them). Or they fill the pages with information that may be significant to them but boring to readers.

Medical doctors start with the patients who need help; that's the principle of book doctors. They take unmarketable manuscripts and revise, edit, or rewrite them. That's the big difference: collaborators start with nothing; book doctors have some kind of manuscript in hand and perform literary surgery.

• • •

I like to watch black-and-white films from the 1930s, and occasionally the opening credits read "Written by XXX." Below that we sometimes see "Additional dialogue by XXX." Recently I saw an old film that said, "Additional dialogue by Ben Hecht." That probably meant that Ben Hecht revised, rewrote, or doctored the original screenplay.

It works the same with books. Sometimes a publisher buys a book based on the reputation of the author or after reading the proposal. When the finished manuscript comes in, they know they can't publish the book the way it is. They drop the whole thing—after investing large sums of money—or they hire someone to do serious reconstructive surgery. That's the work of a book doctor.

Another scenario is when the author works on a manuscript, and before she turns it in, she has doubts about its quality. She shows it to her agent. After reading it, the agent says, "It's not well written. This book needs help." The author hires a book doctor.

A third common problem is that a new author starts writing but can't complete seventy-five thousand words or is wise enough to realize that his book lacks the quality he wants. Instead of going to a ghostwriter, who would probably start all over, he hires a book doctor. Or he might hire a collaborator. However, he may decide that a book doctor can fix the weak places and keep the book essentially intact. Furthermore, it's usually cheaper and faster to hire a book doctor.

Some editors do extensive editing as well, although they wouldn't call themselves book doctors. I know a few in-house editors who end up fulfilling that function as part of their job with their publishers.

One of my friends (who eventually used a book doctor and chooses not to reveal his name), said of his early writing days, "I became so involved in my book, I stayed at it for more than three years." He came home from work and spent two hours every night and most Saturdays devoting himself to writing.

Finally he finished the writing and spent six months polishing it. He bought books on how to format a manuscript and write proposals. Satisfied that his book was as good as he could make it, he printed out the nearly four hundred pages. "It's finished," he told his longsuffering wife and his friends.

After more than a year of trying to sell the book with no editor or agent interested, he was ready to try something else. At a conference, one editor talked to him. "The material is good, and I think it could become a fine book, but the writing doesn't match the quality of the material."

My friend said that, as hard as it was on his pride, it was exactly what he needed to hear. He admits that others had said the same thing in less kind words, but he hadn't been ready to acknowledge his deficiencies.

"I knew about ghostwriters, but I was afraid they'd ruin my voice or insist on putting in their own material." About that time a successful writer talked to him about her first two books. "They were dreadful. If I hadn't hired a book doctor, I would never have gotten published." She admitted that she learned from that expert, and by her third book she no longer hired a doctor. "But I felt I had gone through a graduate-degree course," she added.

"Maybe that's what I need," my friend answered and hired a book doctor. (He did sell the next book, and he has continued to use a book doctor.)

Although book doctors vary in their work, I think of them as those who suggest changes and show the writers how to improve. If hired by the publisher, my understanding is that the book doctor makes the changes and shows them to both the author and the publishing house. When authors hire book doctors, they're under no ethical obligation to name their helper.

Is book doctoring something you think you want to do?

As I see it, if this appeals to you, the most significant need is for you to have the *analytical approach*. I call myself more of an intuitive and find it difficult to examine an entire manuscript and point out repetitions, contradictions, or missing elements. I can do it—and in a few instances, I've done so. Especially in my early years, I doctored four or five books that I've never listed on my resume. It wasn't satisfying work, and for the past decade I've turned down any offers.

The creative writing appealed more to me, where I could start with vague thoughts, creative ideas, and visions, and help authors express their feelings and passion.

My friend Larry Leech is both a book doctor and a ghostwriter/collaborator. When I asked him to define his understanding of book doctor, he wrote, "I see book doctoring as enhancing a manuscript that is just shy of a publishable level. That may entail rewriting sections or occasional sentences, certainly all with the approval of the author. I view ghostwriting and collaborating as handling 100 percent of the writing, again with the approval of the author."

Book doctors, like editors, offer a range of services. The more complicated the material, the more they will charge.

Another book-doctor friend, who works only by referral from previous clients, states, "A simple read-through and proofreading with a comment letter twenty pages long might result in a lower fee, and obviously a complex line-by-line edit costs more.

"As for my fees, it seems impossible to give a range. I charge by the hour, and I make clients pay up front for the hours I estimate I need. If I sense I'll exceed the agreed-upon time, I call to explain the reason and to get approval. Conversely, if I complete the manuscript in less time than I projected, I refund the money. And I've refunded money only four times in my career."

It comes down to this decision for those want-to-publish individuals who just can't get a royalty-paying publisher to offer a contract: they have to decide if they want to take action to increase their chances for publication. Or they can decide that it's too much work to keep trying.

TAKEAWAYS

- Ghostwriter: One who writes a book for another person (author) and receives no byline credit.
- Collaborator: One who writes *with* an author and receives credit. If the word *with* appears before the writer's name, it means that person wrote the book. *And* signifies cowriting.
- As told to: This term is now used mostly in magazines.
- Book doctor: One who takes an already written manuscript and revises or rewrites portions. Some authors credit book doctors in the acknowledgments.

3

Personal Experience, Memoir, and Autobiography

Ghosting isn't limited to writing about the author's personal experience. For example, I wrote several books for Dr. Joel Robertson, a pharmacologist, who specialized in brain chemicals. Three of the books I did with Don Piper (following *90 Minutes in Heaven*) had a purpose other than relating a personal story. My second book with Dr. Ben Carson, *Think Big*, was a motivational book. However, personal experience is what I do most.

So here are several more terms to remember.

Personal experience is a common, cover-all term used in publishing and can mean memoirs, autobiographies, or biographies.

Autobiography obviously refers to the total life of the author up to the present. It's more inclusive and is an attempt to present everything from childhood to the present.

Biography means written in the third person by someone other than the subject of the book.

If I had written a *third-person biography* of Dr. Ben Carson, Franklin Graham, or running back Shaun Alexander, I'm convinced they wouldn't have sold as well.

Think of it this way: biographies are written by someone standing back and looking at the individuals. It's one step removed from the inner personality of the celebrity. Often biographies are written accounts of a life after that person's death.

Memoir refers to a specific period and is based on the author's knowledge of events from personal observation.

Here's the definition from Wikipedia:

Memoir (from French: *mémoire*: *memoria*, meaning *memory* or *reminiscence*) is a literary nonfiction genre. More specifically, it is a collection of memories that an individual writes about moments or events, both public or private, that took place in the author's life. The assertions made in the work are understood to be factual. While memoir has historically been defined as a subcategory of autobiography since the late 20th century, the genre is differentiated in form, presenting a narrowed focus. Like most autobiographies, memoirs are written from the first-person point of view. An autobiography tells the story "of a life," while memoir tells "a story from a life," such as touchstone events and turning points from the author's life. The author of a memoir may be referred to as a *memoirist*.[3]

---

3   http://en.wikipedia.org/wiki/Memoir.

Today most publishers seem to prefer using the fancier word *memoir* for a biography, although it's not technically correct.

TAKEAWAYS

- *Personal experience* is a cover-all term that includes biographies and memoirs.
- *Autobiography*, as the word implies, is someone's life story told from the first person point of view (POV).
- *Biography* is a person's life story told by someone else.
- *Memoir*, although often used for autobiography, refers to a specific period of time or activity and not a person's entire life.

4

ETHICAL QUESTIONS

Do pubs ask themselves diff question than ghostwriter?

When I first began to write for other people, the editor I worked with told me that my name wouldn't appear on the book I was writing. I pondered that situation before I agreed to write.

For me, it was an ethical issue. But as a serious Christian, it was also a spiritual issue. I asked myself, "Am I willing to write the book and not care who receives credit?"

It was the right question for me at that stage of my spiritual development. I wanted my name on the book so people would know I had produced it. It was my work, and I deserved recognition for what I wrote.

About that time I read an article that had been written near the end of the nineteenth century by George Watson called "Others May, You Cannot." Although too long to quote the entire piece, here is the paragraph God used to answer my question:

> Others may boast of themselves, of their work, of their successes, of their writings, but the Holy Spirit will not allow you to do any such thing, and if you begin it,

21

> He will lead you into some deep mortification that will
> make you despise yourself and all your good works.

When I read those words, I received my answer and was satisfied. It didn't matter who received credit from others. God knew; I knew. That was enough.

So I said yes. However, when I listed the books I'd written on my resume, I included them. (My editor assured me that was acceptable.)

That invaluable essay by George Watson allowed me to joyfully write for others. Ego is often a big issue for those of us who want to move into this profession. Those simple words by Watson not only helped shape my attitude, but prepared me for some of the days ahead.

Here's an example involving the ego. At a book signing at the Sweet Spirit Bookstore in Marietta, Georgia, Don Piper graciously invited me to sign alongside him. The people who wanted signatures came to me first, and Don sat on my left. After signing for at least thirty people, I reached out to take the book from one woman, and she pulled it back.

"Who are you? I don't want you touching my book."

I smiled and pointed to my name on the cover.

"Oh. I guess you did have something to do with it," she said. "Go ahead." The last words spoken a bit dismissively seemed to imply, "It can't do much harm."

That incident remains one of my favorite stories, because I think it's hilarious. It also says to me that I had no ego problems over such issues. One of my friends, however, said, "I would have done more than that! I would have explained that I did the writing." He lectured me for several minutes on standing up for myself.

"It just wasn't that big a deal to me," I said, "and I think it's funny."

Once collaborators acknowledge the simple pleasure they derive doing a good job and being compensated for it, the need to see their name on the cover doesn't seem that important. Or perhaps I write only about myself.

If you insist, especially at the beginning, that your name appear on the cover and as large as the author's, collaborating probably isn't for you.

This is just as true using the word *and*. I wrote three books with Don Piper using *and*, although in slightly smaller print. I didn't even notice it wasn't as large until one of my friends called it to my attention. My name did appear on the spine with Don's (again not as big), but it didn't matter.

The ego issue, however, may be a problem on the part of the authors—who might vehemently deny having received help. To my thinking, that speaks more to their insecurity and lack of integrity than it does to anything else.

A few years ago, the mother in a famous country-and-western mother-daughter singing duo, who had recently published their story, appeared on *Good Morning America*. She went through a long explanation of how she had gotten out of bed every morning before daylight, sat down with a cup of coffee, a pen, and her yellow pad, and eventually written the entire book. She went on and on about the demands of the writing process.

Yet the book she held up showed the collaborator's name.

I wonder how her collaborator felt about that interview.

Here's one of my favorite ego stories. My first ghostwriting project was for a famous singer. When we initially met, we had a wonderful time together. He introduced me to a few friends this way: "This is Cec Murphey. He's going to write my book for me."

When I went back a second time, he had read the first one hundred pages of the book and liked what he read. He was proud of the result, and I sensed he was seeing himself a little more involved in the writing. He proved me correct when he introduced me to his pastor: "This is Cec Murphey; he's helping me with my book."

We finished the book a few days before Christmas. My flight out wasn't until early the next morning, so he invited me to a party he and his wife were hosting for a number of musical celebrities. He introduced me to everyone by saying, "This is Cec Murphey. He's a writer."

Just to be clear, I wasn't angry. Because I had worked through my ego issues, it stands among my favorite anecdotes about ghostwriting.

• • •

I don't think the buying public cares whether the author actually wrote the words or someone else did. I've never heard of anyone objecting to our presidents' messages being written by their staff. As long as readers find the book interesting, enjoyable, *and* learn about the celebrity in autobiographies, why would they object?

I will say, however, that most of my ghostwriting opportunities came after my name began to appear on the cover. The first time was in 1990, with *Gifted Hands*, and another big influx came after *90 Minutes in Heaven*.

• • •

I was all right with the arrangement of anonymity for the first dozen years. In 1984, I left the pastorate to write full time, and the same editor I had first worked with provided writing projects for me and increased the flat rate.

Shortly after that two other editors contacted me because they had learned I was a ghostwriter, and my career went forward.

Gifted Hands was the first collaboration for which I received royalties. For the next five years, I vacillated between royalties and flat fees. And since 2000, I've rarely worked on flat-fee projects unless they were about topics that intrigued me.

For example, in 2011, I wrote *The Secret of Enduring Wealth* for Barry Spencer (and my name is on the cover and the same size as his). Not only did I like Barry, but his subject fascinated me. Although far out of my sphere, Barry works with millionaires to show them how to preserve a financial legacy.

• • •

In 1996, for me the question changed from the spiritual to the ethical. I had ghosted a book that won several awards. Afterward the author never thanked me; the publisher never congratulated me. My then agent didn't even acknowledge my work. Perhaps I expected too much, but I thought of words like courtesy and thoughtfulness.

Their lack of acknowledgment led me to the ethical question. As far as the world was concerned, the celebrity had written the book. And that's when I discovered I did have some ego. I might have termed it a question of justice, and I suppose it was that as well.

"Am I helping to perpetuate a deception, even a benign one?" I asked myself. My answer was yes. I was participating in making readers and bookstore personnel assume the author had actually written that book.

About that time my then agent fired me, and in early 1997, I signed with Deidre Knight of The Knight Agency and have joyfully remained with her. The first time we met and she agreed to represent me, she said one thing that endeared her to me: "From now on, you will not write books for other people without your name on the title page."

Except for one difficult female celebrity who verbally promised to give me credit and later refused, we've held to that promise.

• • •

Let's look at the ethics of collaborating. Here are some ideas I've struggled with since 1996.

1. What's the author's purpose? Is it to build up his ego or reputation? I'm not sure we can easily answer that.

One entrepreneur said, "I've conquered just about everything else in my career. Now I'd like to write a couple of best-selling books."

Although I admired his honesty, I chose not to be involved. He did produce books—three or four—and they sold fairly well. I don't know who wrote them, but I know the name of the author.

About the time the ethical issue came up, I heard the late singer George Beverly Shea interviewed on a local radio station. Near the end of the program, almost offhandedly the host said, "And you're also a writer, isn't that so?"

"If you call speaking into a tape recorder and answering questions for someone to write, then I'm a writer."

I loved the honesty of that man.

2. Does the author use the ghostwriter to make her appear more charismatic, brilliant, or insightful than she is? Good writers can do that by adding witty or creative sentences that didn't come out of the mind or mouth of the author, *but* the author left them because she recognized the quality of prose.

I met an author like that one time. I had read two of his nonfiction books and found no coauthor mentioned or acknowledged. Naturally I assumed he had written the books himself, especially after I read the list of people whom he thanked for various reasons.

Then I heard him speak. Any thinking person in that audience should have figured out that he hadn't written the words on the printed page. Even when he read a portion, he stumbled over the sentences. I was disappointed. I wouldn't have minded if he had admitted he'd had help, but he frequently told stories that I later learned had been hatched in the brain of his ghost.

That's what I call dishonest.

Here's a classic case. In 1989, former press secretary Larry Speakes wrote a memoir (in the true sense of the term) called *Speaking Out: The Reagan Presidency from Inside the White House.* His book caused quite an ethical controversy. He stated that many statements purported to be by the president had been either made up or borrowed from other sources.

Shocking perhaps, but that wasn't the cause of the uproar. The president denied the allegations, and several people who knew the truth spoke up for Speakes.

3. What if the author lies to you? It happens. I once wrote a book for a jingles singer who made claims that I didn't question; neither did the publisher. After the book came out, I learned that she had lied about some of the then-famous jingles she purportedly sang as voiceover on TV ads.

I take responsibility for that because it was my job to verify her statements. And that's something I normally do. I'm not excusing my failure, only explaining that she was introduced to me by the publisher as a high-level New York jingles singer. It simply didn't occur to me to check.

The book didn't sell very well, but still, I failed. I also learned—the hard way—that sometimes people enhance their own stories. And if my name is on the cover, as it was on that one, I bear part of the responsibility for the deception.

I did nothing to correct the situation. Right or wrong, I let it go rather than cause problems or embarrass the celebrity. That experience made me promise myself that I'd check facts and not get caught in that situation again.

TAKEAWAYS

- Do you have an ego problem with not being known?
- What ethical issues do you see or foresee?
- What's the author's purpose? Is it to build up his ego or reputation?
- Do the authors use your services to make themselves more charismatic, brilliant, or insightful than they are?
- As much as possible, do you verify facts by the author? (Your answer is yes.)

5

WHY I'M A GHOSTWRITER

As stated earlier, I started my ghostwriting career because an editor said I could do it. Beyond that, after ghostwriting my second book, I knew two things: (1) I could get inside the minds and emotions of others; and (2) I could help those nonwriters express their ideas or stories to share with the world.

That led me to see my role as offering a service *and* performing a ministry. I could translate to the printed page the stories, achievements, and ideas of individuals who'd had marvelous experiences or had unusual insight to share with the world.

Many people have excellent material of amazing stories. Yet they can't open up their own hearts when they write about themselves or topics about which they feel passionate. They tend to skip over the painful memories, sometimes out of the anguish they still dredge up.

That means that for them to get the truth in written form, they need someone else to help them identify their deeper emotions, face those feelings, and convey their anguish on the page. Often they don't even realize significant things about themselves until they try to tell their stories.

Occasionally I work with authors who could have done the writing. That is, they had the talent or could have quickly acquired the needed skills. Immediately I think of Salome Thomas-EL. He's a committed educator who has chosen to work within the inner city. I collaborated with Salome on two books that he could have written himself. *Could have.*

When I stayed at his home in the inner city of Philadelphia, it was easy to grasp why he wouldn't sit in front of his computer and pound out the words. His students loved him, and he genuinely returned the affection. They constantly texted or visited, and he had amazing patience with them. I marveled at the grace he exhibited. But to sit for hours—alone—at a computer—that didn't seem to be within his bag of gifts.

And that's not unusual. Many good public speakers have the same issue. They're smart enough to know that although they can mesmerize with the spoken word, they can't translate that charisma to the page. A number of prominent pulpiteers fit into that category. Blessed are those leaders who are smart enough to know what they don't do well as writers and who hire others. They use their gifts; we use ours.

A second reason I'm a collaborator is that it provides me with an amazing education through the lives of others. I didn't know anything about football until I wrote *Touchdown Alexander.* I didn't know what MRI and CT scans were in 1990, when I wrote *Gifted Hands,* so I had to do research and then explain the machines in a limited number of words. When Don Piper spoke of being fitted with the Ilizarov frame, I had never heard the term before, and Don was, so far as we know, one of the first in the United States to be fitted with one.[4]

---

4   Named after Russian orthopedic surgeon Gavrill Ilizarov, who pioneered a surgical procedure to lengthen or reshape bones in the leg.

Third, I enjoy learning and gaining knowledge, so it's fun for me to write about prison, living ten healthy years longer, or why teens turn to drugs.

Fourth—and this provided the biggest surprise—this style of writing enables me to understand more about Cec Murphey. I learn about others and what goes on inside them, and it translates to learning about myself.

As I grasp the fears, doubts, anxieties, joy, passion, and excitement of the authors, I feel their emotions. Obviously not exactly as they do and often not as deeply, but enough that I learn.

And as I look at myself, I've become more accepting, compassionate, and forgiving of my own failures. As I open myself to hear from God and from others—and I honestly do—I internalize what they say, which enables me to examine how I feel or respond. So I suppose I could call that the selfish aspect of being a collaborator.

Fifth, ghosting challenges me. I stretch my knowledge and delve into the psyches of others. Sometimes I struggle to think and feel like the other person, but I remind myself that, God enabling me, I can do it. In writing, I attempt to pick up the author's speech patterns and way of thinking. I haven't lived in the inner city or in an African-American community, have never been to Siberia, and haven't ever been incarcerated. But I've written about individuals who have.

For example, in 2014, I wrote *Bloodline* for a wonderful man, John Turnipseed. He had been a career criminal whose family had established a kind of black mafia in South Minneapolis. As I listened to John, I learned some of his speech patterns and his way of saying things. I picked up some of the ghetto talk.

I could say the same thing about the book *Stolen: The True Story of a Sex Trafficking Survivor*. Katariina Rosenblatt was trapped in the sex trade three times before God intervened and set her free.

She returned to the trade twice because the traffickers had gotten her addicted to cocaine. And she was susceptible. Her father had been abusive, and she listened to the warm, loving lies of the traffickers and believed them because she wanted to—she needed to feel loved.

Because of my coming from a dysfunctional family with a lot of abuse, I had no trouble feeling Kat's issues and needs. I've never been on any drugs, but through her experiences, I sensed what it was like.

We ghostwriters have the privilege of meeting interesting and fascinating people from various walks of life. And in a limited sense, we share their experiences.

• • •

On a pragmatic level, there are other reasons I'm a ghostwriter.

First, and perhaps most obvious, is that it pays well, especially for those of us who are experienced. I also write my own books, but I derive most of my income by writing for and with other people.

Second, it keeps me productive. Although I'm a man with many ideas, I don't think I could come up with enough good ones to produce at least one book a year. And even if I could, not all of them would pay the bills.

Even after the publishing market took a downturn, I've never been without work. And if you have enough confidence in yourself and can produce at a fairly rapid pace, this might be the career for you.

Third, most of the research comes from the author. I do additional reading so that I always know more than I put on the page. But if I had to do all the research, it would feel endless, because I would start at a place of abysmal ignorance.

By contrast, in 2014, an editor asked me to write a novel based on an upcoming film about the Civil War. I turned him down because it would have taken too much reading and investigating for me.

"There are other writers who can do it easily enough," I said and gave him the name of a good writer who loves that period of American history.

Fourth, ghostwriting helped me establish my reputation as a writer. During the years I was doing anonymous ghosting, no one knew who I was. But once books came out with my name on the cover, even in tiny print, people noticed. In fact, most of my ghostwriting jobs during the 1990s came about because individuals who read *Gifted Hands* contacted me.

Since *90 Minutes in Heaven* came off the press in the fall of 2004, a week has rarely passed in which I haven't gotten at least one query about collaborating. Most of these ideas don't materialize, but several have, or I've passed them on to other ghostwriters I know well.

Fifth, there is a constant demand for collaborators. I hear from people who Googled *ghostwriting* or related words and eventually ran across my name. And this is true with many of my professional friends who do similar work. When people encounter names of cowriters and collaborators and are looking for help, they contact us.

Once publishers and agents know the names and reputations of ghostwriters, they tend to call on them and treat them well. My experience has been that when editors see a book proposal and note that I'm the collaborator, they respond favorably.

Recently, however, my agent forwarded me a rejection from an editor, which made me smile. "We like Cec Murphey's writing, and we're always willing to look at anything by him. Unfortunately, this project just isn't right for us."

Obviously, it's easier for publishers to market books by celebrities or established experts than by unknown writers. For them, the big problem is to make readers aware of the book. The bigger the celebrity, the better the opportunities. If they consider that the scribe behind the star is a good writer, that makes it easier and safer for publishers.

My name as the cowriter *and* a brief paragraph on the inside cover of the dust jacket in hardback or at the back of a paperback enhances the value of the book and also provides me with free advertisement.

Think of it this way. If you were a prospective book buyer and picked up a celebrity-authored book and read the fifty-word bio of the writer, would that influence your decision? Probably, especially if it states that the collaborator's books have appeared on the *USA Today* and *New York Times* best-seller lists.

When collaborators write in the first person, the book promises to get into the inner being of the famous person. By using the words and syntax of the subject, readers can feel they know that person.

One librarian told me, "I love reading and recommending celebrity books written by someone else. Those writers bring things out that the person probably wouldn't."

Something about first person, even though written by someone else, when well done, makes readers forget the writer. At least that's been true for me. For instance, my writer friend Wayne Holmes, a biking enthusiast, suggested I read *It's Not About the Bike*, the first Lance Armstrong autobiography with Sally Jenkins.

"I'm not into biking," I said.

"I know, but I think you'll like Sally Jenkins's writing."

He was right. Jenkins not only writes extremely well, but she has a marvelous ability that made me feel I was inside Lance Armstrong (despite the fact that he later admitted he had lied to her).

I didn't become a fan of Armstrong, but I did become a devotee of Sally Jenkins. She writes for sports figures, and even though I'm not into sports, I read anything by her. Recently I read her book *Sum It Up* by Pat Head Summitt. Women's basketball is far, far down the line of my interests, but Jenkins made me care about Summitt. Thus for me, the book was a great read. I go into that because, in the reading, I forgot that Jenkins was an intermediary. I felt Pat Summitt was showing her transparency, especially with her oncoming dementia.

Another factor is that star names attract readers, and the cult of celebrity has spawned a lucrative niche market for ghostwriters and collaborators. Many, many times consumers don't even notice the *with* line.

Still another plus is that editors expect a certain quality of writing from collaborators. And they should—because that makes less work for them in editing the manuscript.

So far in my career, I've never had an editor ask me for a rewrite or to take a book apart, insisting on a different approach.

I state that because it says I've learned the techniques of writing for this genre.

Collaborating is like being paid for my self-education by a master teacher. I learn directly from the hearts and heads of the experts.

A sixth aspect of being a ghostwriter is that I'm often the go-between for the publisher and the author. The people I write for have busy schedules. Don Piper is the most on-the-road author with whom I've ever worked. He's not always available. Many times the writers can answer the editors' questions or get the information they need quickly.

Some agents work directly with ghosts or send such projects to people on their client list. They do that because they believe they have a book they can sell, but they need a good writer.

If they find a basketball star who's established a fabulous career, they want to get the book to publishing houses while the athlete is still at the top of his game. They don't want to wait until these high scorers have time to write. Usually such athletes have time after their career has ended, but then it's too late. Within three years after they stop playing, few people remember most of the big-name stars that were in the sports news, and publishers are no longer interested.

The same is true of famous personalities of Hollywood's golden era (c. 1930–1960). As an example, in 2009, a once-famous film actress, then in her mid-eighties, asked me to consider writing her autobiography. We met at her spacious home in Universal City. I'm a bit of a film buff and know the names and films of the stars and top character actors from the '30s to the present.

Although the gorgeous actress had appeared in perhaps one hundred films with top stars such as Gregory Peck, Bing

Crosby, Kirk Douglas, and Bob Hope, I didn't think people today would know who she was.

I considered her what I call a changeable leading actress. She was competent, but she didn't appear in any outstanding roles—although she could have done them successfully if she had had a better agent.

As I expected, when I mentioned her name, most people, including editors and my own literary agent, had no idea who she was. Occasionally when friends said, "Oh, yes, I remember that woman," I asked, "Can you name one film in which she starred?"

Only one person, editor-writer Nick Harrison, was able to do that.

As much as I would have liked to tell the actress's story, I turned her down. I made the right decision. At least seven years have passed, and although another writer talked to her, he has not been able to interest a publisher in her autobiography or in her charitable activities.

Seventh, my work provides me a chance to change others' thinking and behavior and to promote causes. For example, one of the reasons I decided to write *Stolen: The True Story of a Sex Trafficking Survivor* for Katariina Rosenblatt was that it was an opportunity to help people understand that sex slavery goes on everywhere, even in small towns across the United States.

• • •

If you would eventually like to become a published author yourself, you may wonder if your writing career will be helped or harmed by ghostwriting. That's a natural concern. My experience has been that instead of hurting, it makes me more valuable. Editors know my work; they know they can depend on me.

However, if the public doesn't know who you are and you move into writing your own books, you may have to start like a beginner—someone who has experience but no platform. While you were giving yourself to your authors, they were promoting their books.

Ghostwriting offers a chance for you to learn how to write professionally, work with editors, and learn a great deal about the publishing world. And you get paid for your efforts—something you may not achieve by starting with your own books. Some important lessons come only from experience and personal connections.

- Ghostwriting gives me access to the lives and insight of others that I would otherwise never have.
- Ghostwriting enables me to enter worlds into which I wouldn't otherwise be invited.
- Collaborating provides a faster turnaround of projects and increases my opportunities to make a living.
- Ghostwriting provides invaluable experience, and I learn more about writing with each book.
- Collaborating gets me known among people within the industry and increases my contacts.
- Collaborating experience increases my chances of getting better advances.
- Ghostwriting implies that the other person has to do the promotional work.
- Ghostwriting in first person can make the stories more dramatic.

• • •

Ghosting is fun and challenging. Every project is different, and I gain so much in writing for others. Most of the time when I work with a person, I feel we connect on a deep level. In a few instances, that person has become a lifetime friend.

My second ghostwriting project was with Stan Cottrell for his book *No Mountain Too High*. Stan is a professional ultra-marathon runner. At the time we met, he had already run across various countries in the world for his organization, Friendship Sports, and averaged fifty miles a day. I tease him now because he's getting old and runs only forty a day.

Stan and I met in 1982, and have been close friends ever since. Sometimes we don't see each other for a couple of months because of our different lifestyles, but within three minutes of meeting again, the time evaporates, and we're back where we were before. My life is richer for knowing and working with high achievers like Stan.

One final reason I'm a ghostwriter: *It's a gift.* I couldn't say that for a long time, but it's true. I was too insecure and unsure of myself that I didn't want to bring dishonor on God by calling it a gift and discovering that editors and readers despised my work.

In 2014, John Turnipseed, the career criminal for whom I wrote *Bloodline*, e-mailed me, "Loved the book, but I may be biased. You even sound like me when I read it. Great job."

Such comments make me *know* I truly have a gift I didn't deserve or earn.

Although it's difficult to write about my gift, I also want to point out that God has endowed all of us with gifts, talents, or abilities—regardless of what we call them. I have come to accept that this is an undeserved present God gave me.

TAKEAWAYS

Let's look at the advantages of being a collaborator or ghostwriter:

- You offer a service *and* perform a ministry.
- This work provides you with an amazing education through the lives of others.
- You learn new skills and gain knowledge about subjects.
- This style of writing enables you to understand yourself better.
- You delve into the psyches of others for greater understanding.

Pragmatic reasons you might want to be a ghostwriter/ collaborator:

- It pays well.
- It can keep you productive, and there's a constant demand for your services.
- Most of the research comes from the author.
- It can help establish your reputation as a writer.
- Editors expect a certain quality of writing from you.
- You often function as the person between the publisher and the author.
- It provides opportunities for you to change thinking and behavior and to promote causes.

6

WHY DO PEOPLE NEED GHOSTWRITERS?

A few months ago I read that 81 percent of people say they have at least one book in them. I don't know how to verify that statement, but it sounds about right.

I respect those who ask people like me to be their collaborator. It takes courage and honesty to admit, "I can't do it." It also indicates that the person is a doer rather than a dreamer. Dreamers talk about the book they plan to write or mention the one they've been working on for five years and never finish.

Wise doers hire ghostwriters because they recognize that since their book isn't getting written, they need to find another way to get it done. That takes enormous strength of character, especially from high-achieving individuals.

The first and most obvious reason people want someone to write their book is that they're experts in their particular field, or they've had powerful experiences and feel their stories need to be told, but they recognize they can't write.

That doesn't mean they don't try before they contact me—they often do. They respect me more because of their failed attempts. More than once I've written for individuals who have handed me a mammoth-sized manuscript and apologetically admitted, "I know it's not very good."

The first time that happened, the author had about seven hundred pages of single-spaced material, and an editor at Thomas Nelson/HarperCollins asked me to take over the project.

"Lose your manuscript," I told him. "It's bogged down with facts and irrelevant material for readers." He did exactly that and allowed me to start by taping relevant material. We turned out a book that sold quite well.

• • •

When I'm asked by a professional to ghostwrite, I sometimes think of Irwin Shields. I met him when I was sixteen and harbored a secret desire to write. We became friends (or at least I adopted him as one) after he told me, "I'm a writer."

Irwin went on to talk about the novel he was writing. That excited me, and I asked many questions, but he refused to tell me or anyone what was in it. He was afraid someone would steal his plot.

I did learn that Irwin had quit his teaching job two years after completing college and moved from St. Cloud, Minnesota, to Davenport, Iowa, where I lived. If he told me the reason he had chosen Iowa, I don't remember. He lived in a one-room apartment and worked on one book for ten years.

By then he had depleted his savings, deprived himself of food and medical care, and developed lung cancer, and some people who knew him paid his bus fare to return to St. Cloud. We later learned that Erwin died only months after his return—and his book wasn't published.

As I thought of him years later, I wondered why he hadn't used his savings to hire a ghostwriter. Or at least a book doctor.

• • •

One of the major reasons speakers want to hire me is that they know they can earn more money and get wider publicity if they have at least one book to sell at the back of the room. They get interviewed because of it, and that increases their recognition.

"Having you write for me was the best step I made toward getting more speaking engagements," one author said to me. "If people don't know much about me but are interested, I mail them a free copy of my book. My speaking has increased dramatically."

Some organizations, companies, and associations view published authors as safe choices when they seek a speaker. If the book is well written and sounds like the speaker, it functions as their audition.

Also the person recommending the speaker can say, "She has a book out." It's something tangible to add to the qualification.

As one prominent author with twelve ghosted books behind him said, "My books are my best single piece of promotional material."

• • •

Some people will never publish without a collaborator. I've heard various figures (without being able to verify them), but several times I've been told that each year two to five million manuscripts go to publishers, and only about 1 percent end up in print.

Accurate or not, the point is that getting published isn't easy. Few people (perhaps none) have a natural, innate ability to write and sell a first book without help.

Editors are overworked, and the demand for them to produce grows more intense. They no longer have time to give books a careful rewrite or extensive editing. Stated another way, why wouldn't they want to have a professionally written manuscript from which to start?

Many brilliant individuals can't write; famous public speakers freeze when they face a computer screen. A few of them are smart enough to know that writing's not a talent they possess, so why spend time on something that's not productive?

These people make the best clients because they're accustomed to turning to experts—people they know can do the job they want accomplished.

The most difficult authors are those who think they're writers and want only "a little help" and become argumentative over every suggestion. I've wondered why they come to us ghostwriters if they can't accept what we write for them.

I also think of those who are gifted speakers with no interest in learning the craft of writing. They realize the power of the written word and want to be able to sell books at the end of their meetings. That's an excellent reason for hiring a ghostwriter.

• • •

Another reason people need ghostwriters is that many could (possibly) write their own material, but they say, "I don't have time." That answer probably means that time spent in writing a book isn't among their top priorities. They're good at what they do and need to do more of it; too many people who can't write waste their time trying and will probably never finish the project.

This is probably obvious, but these prospective authors have gifts and may be quite successful in their chosen fields, but they're unable to write books.

• • •

A number of professional speakers give writers transcripts of their messages and ask them to turn them into a book. One time I tried working from CDs—only once. I knew the famous pastor well, and his personal assistant sent me twelve CDs. That book turned out to be one of the hardest collaborations I've ever done.

Although I knew it in theory, I learned through experience the vast difference between oral and written communication. While working from the CDs, I realized that his sermons were most effective when he repeated points or referred to them again. After going through the twelve CDs, I didn't have enough information for a full book.

I had good material, but I had either to insert my own or ask him for more. I called him and discussed the situation, and he said, "Go ahead and add whatever you think fits."

I did. He liked it. And I was happy to fill in the holes of the book. But it was still more work than most of the projects I've done.

• • •

I've never seen this mentioned, but I'm convinced it's true: authors say they can't *spend the time alone* that writing demands. Their trouble is not only the time factor, but being by themselves, isolated from others.

To write a book that touches, encourages, motivates, or excites people means the authors have dipped deeply inside themselves. They've faced their own heartaches or perhaps what we call the dark night of the soul. For significant impact, the author has to go through serious self-examination, and that's often difficult.

Not everyone can do soul searching or introspection on their own. A good ghostwriter elicits those deeper feelings and can listen to an author with empathy *and with objectivity.*

The most difficult book I ever had to write wasn't ghosted. It was called *When a Man You Love Was Abused.* I wrote it to help women understand men who had been victimized in their childhood by sexual predators. I'm a survivor and had been dealing with the effects of my abuse for at least ten years. Before I began writing about it, I assumed I was past the pain.

How wrong I was. Many times I had to wipe away tears as I opened myself to put words on paper. A few times I was so emotionally distraught at reliving the past that I left my computer and went for a long walk. At least twice I had to stop writing for a full day so I could work through newly felt emotions.

I'm convinced that working with and trying to understand others through my collaborating was a large factor in being able to write that book.

• • •

Needing a ghostwriter is not just a matter of inability in want-to-write authors. Several times I've said to individuals, "I've seen talent in what you've shown me, but you don't have the skills. You can develop the expertise to write well, but that's not something you pick up in six months." Most of them don't want to go through the torturous route of learning to write.

Although several people have told me similar anecdotes, the following happened to me in 2011, at a writers conference in Atlanta.

After a chiropractor and I chatted, he said, "You know, I've been thinking about taking off a few months and writing my novel."

"How interesting. I've been thinking about taking the summer off to learn to be a chiropractor."

"But you can't learn it that quickly—" He stopped and grinned. "I get it."

I'd heard such stories for years, but it was the first (and so far only) time when someone has talked to me about taking "a few months" to become a writer.

• • •

Another reason for hiring a collaborator is that the authors are too close to the subject. It's often difficult to write about the things we know best—especially among non-writers. When individuals have shown me their manuscripts, the books are filled with details that might be important to them but are of no interest to readers. Or they assume readers know the same things they know and that anyone in the world will understand their language.

For example, before I collaborated on two business books, I had no idea what ROI [return on investment] or HR [human resources] meant, so I had to ask. Perhaps those terms are fairly well-known, but there are always individuals like me who raise an eyebrow and wonder, "What does that mean?" Or they miss the meaning or purpose of the sentence.

• • •

The single biggest problem with untrained authors trying to put out their own book is their lack of emotional input. They may feel anger or love, be depressed or ecstatic, but they don't know how to *show* readers. To simply say, "I was angry," doesn't communicate very much. "I wanted to punch him in the face," expresses anger.

Experienced collaborators also bring perspective to books. Even though we normally write in first person, we're conscious of writing from the *readers'* point of view. Because of our background and experience, we sense the things that detract from or resonate with readers. We cut the mundane and include the exciting.

Not only do ghostwriters need experience, we have to be able to grasp the author's perspective on life and become aware of what's important to that person. One problem I've noticed is where authors look to find their writers. Too often sports figures want writers in their own field, and that's not always wrong. But I contend that good collaborators will normally do better *because of their ignorance.* They'll ask the questions readers might ask.

When I wrote *Touchdown Alexander,* I knew very little about football. I know more now because Shaun Alexander would say things like, "And then we had a bye that week," and I'd have to ask him to explain. Most sportswriters would rightly assume that almost anyone who knows football would understand. *Almost everyone.*

I write for the ignorant readers so they'll know that field better. That is, I ask questions that people not involved in the sports world might ask (or those who need to have the terms clarified). Even some who watch football may not clearly understand terms such as *double wing formation* or the *wheel route*.

Put another way, I'm seminary trained, and if I filled my prose with theological terms like *supralapsarian* or urged people to flee concupiscence, would they know what I meant?

• • •

Many times the author doesn't have the self-discipline to complete the project. I'm aware of countless times where individuals start a book, get one third of the way through, and lose interest. They start with great energy but eventually see it as tedious and, if they're honest, admit they can't do it. That's when they seek people like me for help.

Another point I want to make is that, especially when writing personal experience books, some individuals hire a ghost when they're really seeking a therapist—even though they don't know it, and I don't tell them. Sometimes I think of my work as that of a shrink. Once authors trust me, they unburden their souls—and later comment how much better they feel.

In my early freelance days, I wrote a book for an entrepreneur whom I liked. When he told me the short version of his story, I was touched but warned, "You might not be able to sell it."

"It'll sell," he said confidently.

I wrote the book. It didn't sell, but by then he was satisfied that he had exorcised his personal demons.

Although I wouldn't do that again, I realize that it's easier for most people to talk about themselves and their passion for several hours than to sit in front of a computer for months to achieve the same results.

● ● ●

Never underestimate the vanity angle.

Some people want to make a name for themselves. They feel that if they have a book, it makes them significant.

In 1999, I met Carl (and I'm delighted I can't remember his last name) at a writers conference in Delaware. He was positive that I was the man to write his book. "I've been told you're the best," he said, "and I'm willing to pay."

Carl pressured me for weeks after the conference, and I finally told him that if he wanted to come to Atlanta, I'd set aside a few hours to hear him out.

Carl visited, and from a huge suitcase he pulled out charts, pictures, and several three-dimensional visual aids.

I'm not sure I understood what he was trying to say. Repeatedly I questioned him because I couldn't grasp a clear concept from which to work.

Finally I said, "Carl, focus your eyes on me, and don't move them until you answer this question: "Why do you want to write a book?"

After what seemed like a full minute of intense gazing, tears filled his eyes. "So I can be somebody."

"You already are somebody," I said and tried to explain that having a book wouldn't make him more important.

Years later I saw Carl at a trade show in Orlando. He ran up to me, hugged me, and showed me a copy of his self-published book. "I finally did it!"

Carl didn't give me a copy but hurriedly paged through the book, showing me some of the same graphs and pictures he had brought to my house. I did read the first page. The essence of his book seemed to be, "Because Jesus willingly sacrificed himself, we're free from sin."

Maybe I had been too dense when he showed me his graphs and charts to grasp that simple concept.

• • •

In our culture there's a mystique about being "a real writer." I think of the intimate connection between the eyes and the page. Someone said, "It's as if your words make little explosions in readers' minds."

That translates into the reality that people identify with and feel a kinship to the authors of books they like and will buy others they've written—which builds a fan base.

Often after I speak publicly and talk with people who buy books, I hear these words: "I've never met a real writer before."

When I state that I write others' books, immediately I add, "I'm not looking for work." Until I started doing that, almost every time, one or two individuals would wait to talk with me after I finished. Their beginning statement was often, "I've lived such an interesting life."

That's probably true, but that doesn't mean they need to write about it or that anyone would want to read their history. I don't want to hurt their feelings, so sometimes I tell them,

"That sounds like a great idea for a family history or legacy for your family. Self-publishing is probably the way to go."

• • •

Another attraction for coming to ghostwriters like me is that authors, especially first-timers, seek my contacts and experience. For them, my connections seem more important than my writing ability.

Unless they already have an agent or business manager, they usually know nothing about the publishing industry. They feel they have a unique story or a powerful book, but they don't know where to send it or how to approach an agent or publisher. And it makes sense that the more experienced the collaborator, the better the chances of placing a book.

Authors need to believe they have something of interest to say to people who will read their book. Some individuals are so narcissistic they assume that if they think their lives or thoughts are interesting, thousands of others will feel the same way.

Publication also helps authors in other areas. Having a published book can be a good marketing tool. I've heard that some speakers earn more dollars from their book tables than they do from traditional outlets.

Another factor in seeking out collaborators is that potential authors know they can rely on the professionalism of ghostwriters. They want a book to come back to them in proper format, content, and length, and following the promises given in the proposals.

If the authors aren't professionals, it usually means the manuscripts will need collaborators to produce an exceptional book.

TAKEAWAYS

People need and hire ghostwriters because:
- Authors recognize that their books aren't getting written, so they find another way to get it done.
- Speakers know they can earn more money and get wider publicity if they have at least one book.
- People know they're experts in their field or have had powerful experiences yet are accustomed to turning to experts—people who can accomplish the job they want done.
- Many authors could (possibly) write their own material, but that's not high on their list of priorities. They can't or won't spend the time alone that writing demands.
- Authors' reluctance isn't only about the time factor but about being by themselves, isolated from others.
- They have the talent to write but not the skills and won't spend years going through the torturous route of learning to write.
- Authors may be too close to the subject. It's often difficult to write about the things they know best.
- Experienced collaborators bring their experience and professional perspective to books.
- Authors don't have the self-discipline to complete the project.
- When seeking to write about personal experiences, some individuals are unknowingly looking for a therapist.
- People want your contacts and experience. Unless they already have an agent or business manager, they usually know nothing about the publishing industry.

- Publication helps authors in other areas, and having a published book can be a good marketing tool.

7

TURNING SERMONS INTO BOOKS

If you choose to work with a preacher, consider the sermon message a rough draft—an extremely rough draft. It's vastly different writing for the eye than for the ear. Because I was a pastor for fourteen years (and a part-time writer during most of that time), here's my perspective.

Aside from the power of repetition, when we preach, our voices are primary, and our enthusiasm can make weak sermons sound profound. We can get away with using only biblical illustrations. By pausing or using body language, no one notices weak transitions.

Sermons are naturally biblically based. The problem is that many of them sound like preaching—that is, too much is telling and not showing. (Too many homilies begin with something like, "As John tells the story of the feeding of the five thousand in chapter 6 of his Gospel . . .") They have a captive audience, and many pulpiteers don't think about grabbing and holding people's attention.

When we write, however, we have only the printed page. We need a hook to grab readers. Each chapter needs a single focus, even if we illustrate it with five points. Every illustration needs to center on the focus. We avoid redundancies. If readers don't get something, they only have to look back at the previous pages.

• • •

When we transition from an oral message to a book, we need to remember several things.

1. We have to earn the right to be read. Our words need to promise something of value, not only when potential buyers pick up the book, but each time they open it.

With sermons, as we all know, some are better than others. People don't stop going to a church when they hear one ineffectual sermon. But one bad chapter of a book is enough for people to stop reading and banish the book to a giveaway pile.

2. We have to think about length in a different way. In sermons we face a time constraint. The old saying of three points and a poem may hold true, but instead of going the traditional forty-five minutes, the allotted time today is shorter.

Print length has to do with word count. Thirty years ago a chapter could easily run five thousand words. Not many writers get away with that length now unless they have a number of page breaks. I work on the principle of the economy of words. I suggest you rarely exceed two thousand words in your chapters.

3. We have to be consistent with the viewpoint. Generally it is good to choose first-person singular or plural. Or we may use second person. In sermons, our ears don't catch those shifts.

Here's my rule. If I'm telling you my own experience and preference, obviously I use first-person singular. When I want to be inclusive (as I've done with each of the points in this section), it's first-person plural. But when I want to write as the instructor, I revert to *you*, the second person.

4. We have to shift from the local to the universal in print. Good sermons illustrate the points using situations and individuals who are prominent in a church or community or presently in the news. A pastor may say, "The tragic shooting in Peachtree City needs to be a lesson to us." That's an obvious reference to a current situation, but by the time the book is in print, the reference likely means nothing.

If we want to use the same story, we have to go into detail so that readers in Nome, Alaska, or Bayonne, New Jersey, will understand. And we have to be sure the message has a broader appeal than to the 227 members of a congregation.

5. We have to avoid filling our books with biblical quotations. Most preachers have a Scripture reading before they preach. In many congregations they use both Old Testament, New Testament, and Psalms—often read at different places during the worship hour.

In print, we don't get away with that today. I realize that many books still come off the press with a Bible verse or two at the beginning of each chapter. My theory (and I've asked dozens of people who confirm this) is that Christian readers usually glance at the reference and think, "Oh, I know that," and they skim past it.

I try to put Bible verses in the middle of paragraphs and keep them as short as possible to retain the meaning. Further, I keep verses to a minimum because I don't want a string of proof texts. (Yes, there are appropriate exceptions.)

• • •

The most serious problem for turning sermons into print is getting rid of the preachiness or sermonic tone. Perhaps the best way to explain is by using my own journey. When I was a new pastor and an amateur author, I wrote my conclusion of a then-proposed chapter called "Bargaining with God" this way:

> God is the One who gives abundantly and freely. We need not bargain or force God to do something contrary to himself. He blesses, for that is his nature. Our task is to put ourselves in line with his will. We live in gratitude, our lives filled with thanksgiving for his "favors freely bestowed." Neither our gratitude nor our obedience gets prayers answered. The means is God himself.

Yes, it's awful. Notice the stiff, formal language ("We need not . . ."). Did you "hear" the preacher sounds—statements and pronouncements?

- *We live in gratitude*
- *Our lives are filled with thanksgiving*
- *Neither our gratitude*

I didn't sell the book, but I kept it in my files. In 1997, I revised the chapter and sold the book. Here's how I changed that paragraph:

After twenty-five years of being a Christian, I've finally learned that we don't have to beg or try to force God to answer us.

TAKEAWAYS

If you choose to work with preachers, especially your own pastor, be aware that writing for the eye differs vastly from writing for the ear.

This is information you can pass on to potential clients:

- Hiring a good ghostwriter takes away the stress of trying to produce an excellent book.
- Most people don't know how to structure a book.
- Many successful people don't have the time or interest in writing a book themselves.
- Even if prospective clients have the talent, they can't or won't spend three years learning the craft.
- Many don't have the self-discipline to finish the project.

If you turn lectures or sermons into books, here are things to remember:

- Your book must earn the right to be read.
- Think about length in a different way.
- Be consistent with the viewpoint.
- Learn to shift from the local to the universal.
- Avoid filling your manuscripts with biblical quotations.

8

WHAT YOU NEED TO BECOME A GOOD GHOSTWRITER

Contrary to what some imply, not every good writer can become a ghostwriter. Ghostwriting is hard work, and you need special talent to do it. *And the temperament.*

If you choose to try your skills at ghostwriting or collaborating, here are things to keep in mind.

As a ghostwriter, you become invisible. Readers don't want to hear your voice, know your opinions, or read your style. They buy the book because of the author.

You can enable authors to interpret their experiences or clarify their perceptions so readers understand their intended meaning.

Sometimes you can help them reflect on or grasp the power of an experience in their lives. Years ago I worked with Lida Vashchenko, one of the Siberian Seven, who defied the Kremlin during the Cold War. Seven members of two families converged on the American embassy in Moscow and lived in a room ten feet by ten feet. If they left the embassy, they knew they would be imprisoned, tortured, and possibly killed.

After five years Lida went on a fast, ready to die unless the administration relented. The then-Soviet government capitulated and set her free.

After we worked together she told me about the events of her life behind the Iron Curtain. It was mostly a litany of actions. "I did this, and then I went . . ."

"Wait a minute before you go on," I probably said a dozen times. I asked a few questions, and each time a puzzled look came over her face.

"Ah, yes, just now I understand the lesson from that experience."

I didn't give her the comprehension; I merely provided the pause and the opportunity for her to explain something *to herself.*

You need to be able to grasp the theme and structure of a story from among the many things the author tells you; they may not know the real theme. Along with that comes the ability to ask the right questions and at the proper time.

• • •

You need to listen—really listen. The first time my transcriber, Wanda Rosenberry, heard the tapes of my interviews, she e-mailed me, "You don't say much, do you?"[5]

That was the point. A collaborator listens. I often say that I pay more attention *to the person* than to the words spoken.

This may sound obvious, but many people don't realize how often they offer advice or interrupt.

---

5   Wanda Rosenberry, wandarose38368@hotmail.com.

A few years ago I sat alone in my office and listened to the transcript of a forty-five-minute TV interview with someone about whom I was going to write.

"He talks too much!" I shouted, referring to the host.

I'm no therapist, but I felt the host was trying too hard to impress his guest or his audience. Or perhaps he was simply unsure of himself. Even when he asked simple questions, the host phrased them two or three different ways before giving the man a chance to respond.

In his interview, the guest related an incident about his car being stopped by robbers at gunpoint. He was telling about the fear that clutched at him and said something like this: "But my protective love for my children enabled me to face those criminals."

"How many children do you have?"

"What?" I yelled at the transcription. The host ruined the story and destroyed the impact by asking a question that wasn't relevant to that illustration. He could have asked about the number of children earlier or later but not in the middle of a life-or-death situation.

Another problem is that collaborators can push their own agenda. For a short time I lived in Louisville, Kentucky. A feature writer from the *Courier-Journal* asked to interview me about being a ghostwriter. We had a delightful time together, but three times he made comments like, "And you'd rather have the money than the fame."

"Neither of them are my issues," I said.

A few days later the article appeared on the front page. He did a good job and accurately portrayed me until the last paragraph. His last sentence read, "As a ghostwriter, Murphey would rather have the money than the fame."

• • •

Another thing about collaboration—and this is more common than I assumed—is that people want to offer advice. Unless ghostwriters guard themselves, they'll fall into the habit of trying to solve the authors' problems. I've discovered over the years that too many people, especially our friends, load us down with their opinions, suggestions, and recommendations without realizing it or whether it's wanted.

For example, around 2008, a group of us writers met monthly for lunch and shared our struggles and successes. Three of us were ghostwriters. On one particular Friday, I said, "I'm struggling with something, and I'd like you to listen. I don't want advice, I need to articulate it." I added, "Sometimes I have to hear my own words before I know what I think."

They laughed. Then I explained a situation in which I found myself with a demanding author. I had hardly paused before the other six people there began throwing out advice. *Every one of them.*

For a few minutes I listened and said nothing. Finally I said, "I told you I didn't need advice. I just needed to be heard."

One or two apologized, and almost immediately after that one of them offered additional advice to help me cope with my dilemma. Realizing it was futile, I smiled and said, "Thanks for listening." I don't think they heard the sarcasm in my voice.

Here's an aphorism I wrote in memory of that day: a true friend knows all about me, still loves me, *and has no plan for my self-improvement.*

When I write, I remind myself of my maxim and keep quiet. As ghostwriters, our role isn't to instruct, guide, or correct. As

I've shown from the two examples, we're responsible to get the facts and listen to the heart of the author.

• • •

You also honor confidentiality. One of the first things I say to a client is, "I promise you I will never tell anything about you without your permission." That may not be necessary, but all but one author I've worked with has at some point said, "I've never told anyone this before . . ." or, "I'd like you to understand this, but I don't want it in the book."

I assure them that I'll guard their secrets.

• • •

Think of ghostwriting as your spiritual or humanitarian service. You took on the project because you felt the person had a story to tell or insights to offer. Besides autobiographies, I've written on diet and health, exercise, finances, dealing with drugs, attempted suicides, and incarceration.

Ghostwriters must have the capacity to feel empathy. I don't know how to say it any other way. You have to be able to get inside the heart of the person for whom you write so you can understand and sympathize, even if you think the person made a foolish or wrong decision.

Empathy is more important than most people recognize or admit. When people talk to me and tell me they would make good ghostwriters, my first statement is usually something like this: "To be a good ghostwriter, you need to be able to get inside other people's heads."

"I can do that," is the usual breezy answer.

When they say those words, my immediate silent response is, "You probably can't." Getting inside others isn't easy and requires skill that many people—even some successful ghostwriters—don't have.

Although I admit that my experience isn't the same as everyone else's, it took me years to understand that I could get inside others, something Victor Oliver had seen immediately.

I admire writers who know they can't get inside others. Years ago my late friend Suzanne Stewart wrote two highly successful books, and the publisher asked her to ghostwrite *Joni*, which was the Joni Erickson Tada story. Without hesitating, Suzanne turned them down, saying she didn't know how to write for other people.

Another friend, Marion Bond West, is *Guideposts'* most published writer (and she'll tell you she's also their most rejected). When asked to ghostwrite for others, she knew that wasn't her forte, and like Suzanne, she said no. However, she admitted, "I ghosted a few articles that I felt strongly about and was emotionally moved to write."

Another way to say it is that if you want to become a ghostwriter, you need to see life and circumstances through another's eyes. As you hear people, can you feel their pain? Their exuberance? Unless you, the writer, can admit to strongly deep, powerful emotions, especially what we refer to as negative feelings, I don't think you can get inside their heads.

The first time I realized I had that ability was after I wrote for Lida Vashchenko, whom I mentioned. She had lived in an oppressive society where she could rarely talk to outsiders about feelings. When working with her, I'd listen to a story—often told factually—and then I'd say, "What was going on inside you? How did you feel about what he did?"

"I don't know," she would answer in her thick accent. I believe she told the truth.

As I worked on the book, I regularly asked myself, "How would she feel?" "What did she think?" Because she wasn't able to help me, I wrote the best I could. After I finished the entire manuscript, I mailed it to her.

A week after receiving the completed book, Lida phoned. Her first words were, "How did you know? That's exactly how I felt, although I didn't realize it until I read the words."

Talented ghosts develop those skills because we focus attention on understanding the other person. Here's how I say it: "I record the data—the information—but I need to absorb the emotions by watching and listening."

• • •

Perhaps it's not necessary to say this, but some writers can never be good collaborators because they won't allow someone to have a discordant opinion. They behave as if they have some special, holy anointing to correct every unorthodox thought.

So how do I work with someone whose philosophy or theology doesn't agree with mine? At one time I worked with a man who was convinced he knew God's plan for the end of time and believed Russia was the Antichrist. I didn't agree with many of his theological positions, but he hadn't hired me to teach. Had I known he felt so adamantly, I might have turned him down.

But because I had signed a contract, my role was to communicate *his* theology. (When the Berlin Wall fell in 1989, he was devastated and had to rethink his theology, so we didn't finish the book.)

Not everyone can put away opinions or biases. And yet professionals know they're paid to provide what the author wants, even if they strongly disagree. If they can't do that, they need to break the contract.

Never forget that authors pay *you* to perform a task. Your responsibility is to do what they ask. That is, they pay you to correctly explain their perspective.

A writer friend challenged me on that position because he knew I didn't agree with something I had written for one author. He charged, "You compromised."

"No, I don't think so," I said. "My role was to communicate what *he* believed, and I did that."

"I couldn't write that heresy!"

"Which is a good argument," I said, "on why you shouldn't try to become a ghostwriter."

I felt strongly on that point and still do. A good ghostwriter leaves no indication of being involved in the writing. If the book is to sound like the author, it means for the collaborator, "Hands off your own opinion."

I tell prospective ghostwriters, "Your role is to listen uncritically and write from the author's point of view."

You need to put away your own opinions—even if you're convinced your author is wrong. If you have intense feelings about a book, don't agree to write, or opt out of the contract. Furthermore, readers aren't interested in you or your perspective; they buy the book because of the author's thoughts or expertise.

TAKEAWAYS

Here's a list of qualities you need if you want to become a successful collaborator.

- Be an already published writer and know how to pace a book to keep it flowing and interesting.
- Be able to understand the sound and rhythm of words.
- Surprise your readers by creating suspense, and make them wonder what's coming next. Don't be predictable.
- Write for scanners as well as those who never miss a word. In several of my books I've used callouts—a sentence or two from the text that encapsulates the theme of the chapter. In this book, there are brief statements for scanners at the end of each chapter.
- Inject emotion into your writing, even for self-help and business books.
- Become comfortable in interviewing others. That is, guide the interview and extract necessary details that may be emotionally upsetting or embarrassing for the author to recall. And do it with compassion.
- Don't judge the clients for what they've done or haven't done.
- Remove yourself from the writing and, in effect, become the author during the creative process—the same way actors do with the characters they portray. Discover and capture the author's voice, and write with the emphasis, rhythm, and style of that personality, not your own.
- Know how to edit yourself, but be aware when it's time to have someone else edit your writing.
- Be able to accept someone else's suggestions without becoming defensive or angry.

As a ghostwriter:
- Become invisible.
- Enable authors to interpret their experiences or clarify their perceptions so readers understand what's intended.
- Grasp the theme and structure of a story from among the many things the author tells you.
- Have the ability to ask the right questions at the right time.
- Listen—more *to the person* than to the words spoken.
- Don't push your own ideas.
- Don't offer advice. Your role isn't to instruct, guide, or correct.
- Honor confidentiality.
- Consider ghostwriting as your spiritual or humanitarian service.
- Get inside the hearts of the people for whom you write.

9

WHAT ELSE YOU NEED TO BECOME A GOOD GHOSTWRITER

Here are *subjective* questions if you want to move into ghost-writing as a career.

First of all, are you a self-starter? Self-disciplined? Can you meet deadlines? These questions apply to many kinds of writing, of course, but they're extremely important when it comes to collaborating. You have to be able to take the initiative and keep the work going.

A senior editor once contacted me to do ghostwriting for his house, and we did at least a dozen projects together. Many years later I learned why he threw so much work my way.

His house had previously used another ghostwriter who was excellent (and in all candor, a better writer than I was) but didn't know the meaning of the word *deadline*. In the ten years she had ghosted for them, the editor said, "Not once was she ever on time. She caused problems in our scheduling. We finally figured out that in order to work with her we had to give her a deadline two months before we needed the manuscript."

Any wonder they threw work my way? I was dependable and did what they asked. *And* I never missed a deadline.

I stress this for several reasons.

First, of course, is that publishers shouldn't have to check up on their writers to see if the book will meet the deadline.

Second, doing the work well and having it finished in time is a mark of professionalism. A number of editors complain about the slowness of writers in getting the work done on schedule *and according to the signed contract.*

When we sign a contract, one of the statements in there gives the due date. And that date is when you, the collaborator, agree to have the book to the publishing house and no later.

In 1989, an editor at Thomas Nelson asked me to write *The Dictionary of Biblical Literacy.* It was a reference book, and they sent me several books as research material. There was one catch: "We need it in sixty days."

"That's impossible," I said, "but I'll do it."

And I did, although I doubt that I'd ever take on such an assignment again. I worked an average of fourteen hours a day, six days a week and Sunday afternoons. When I sent my manuscript to them, it was sixteen hundred pages long. I also beat my deadline by one day.

Except for three instances, whenever I've worked with a royalty-paying publisher, I'm the one who has decided when I could deliver a completed manuscript. It's normally a point of negotiation. In a few instances, the editor has said something like, "If you get this to us by September 1, we can put it in our spring catalog."

The way it usually works, after an editor tells my agent, "We want to make an offer," my agent consults me before saying yes. Then she and the editor negotiate. After they agree on the finer points of the contract, such as royalty and foreign and film rights, they discuss the length of the book and when it's due.

Unless the offer contains a date by which they need to have the manuscript, when my agent notifies me of the pending offer, she asks me when I'll be able to complete the work.

From experience, I have a sense of how long it will take me to write the book, so I set the date. I usually ask for about a month longer than I think I'll need. That's because all authors aren't equal in responding to me.

Some of them, like Ben Carson, Salome Thomas-EL, or Katariina Rosenblatt, provided quick responses. Although I did four books with Don Piper, the turnaround was slow, and the major reason was that he travels almost constantly. He mentioned a few weeks ago that he still speaks about two hundred times a year, so he's not able to get everything back so quickly.

Others, like John Turnipseed, are what I call the middle ground. They read over what I've sent them, possibly two or three times, and are more methodical and slower.

I need to make allowances for the fast, slow, and middle-ground authors. Unless I already know the person well, I try to build in extra time for the slow response.

What some collaborators don't realize is that once they sign the contract, the publishing house puts the book on their assembly line. Only one publisher has ever sent me the schedule, which was early in my career, and it helped me grasp the significance of holding to my agreed-on deadline.

Occasionally a publisher has said, "We have to have this done by _____." If I thought I couldn't do it, that would be my time to speak out.

In 2014, Carlton Garborg of BroadStreet Publishing Group offered me a contract. I know the publisher well, having worked with him when he was with a different company. In February, Carlton said, "If you can have this to us by June 1, we can push this so it's off the press in October.[6] However, if you can't get it to us by then, we'll delay it until our spring catalog and will need it by December 1."

I stress all this because true professionals meet their agreed-on deadlines.

Only twice in nearly 140 books have I missed a deadline. The first time, the musician about whom I was writing, went to China for a month. The second time, the author was extremely busy, even though he had agreed with me on the date. When he fell behind, I told him, "You need to contact our editor and explain that you're unable to give me the material I need to meet the deadline." I was serious about his accepting responsibility for the delay. (He did tell them, and the editor gave us a month's reprieve, which we met.)

Editors appreciate writers who meet the contract deadlines.

• • •

Second, can you treat collaboration as a business? Writing is an art, a craft, and anything else we want to call it. When we sign a contract, we're engaged in a business enterprise. For some of us, this is a form of ministry to God, but it's still a business.

---

6   It's rare to have such a quick manuscript delivery-to-print agreement.

Once you set up your business enterprise, you need to keep good records and receipts. You can usually get tax credits for your expenses. But to do that, you need accurate records. My policy is that if I don't have a receipt, I can't give myself credit.

• • •

A third thing to consider is, do you get along with people? Perhaps I shouldn't have to ask that question, but one sad experience has made me cautious. I knew a somewhat successful writer whom I'll call Mel. He was more of an acquaintance, but I had read and liked his nonfiction books.

One day when Mel and I had lunch together, he told me that he had decided he should become a ghostwriter. "I've been pondering this for months, and I'm convinced this is the new path for me to take." He leaned over, lowered his voice, and said, "Would you mind sending some work my way?"

While I was trying to figure out how to respond, he said, with a slight edge to his voice, "You're not afraid of the competition, are you?" Then he smiled.

I shook my head. Something about the way he asked that question troubled me, but I pushed it off as just his way of joking.

About a week after that, I received an opportunity to write a book for someone. I knew it wouldn't be a big seller, but I thought it was a good project. However, the editor wanted the book done quickly and couldn't wait for me.

"Sorry, I can't squeeze it in," I said to the editor, "but do you know Mel? He's published three books and wants to be a ghostwriter."

He knew of him and said, "Okay, I'll give him a chance at this."

The editor followed through; Mel called and thanked me profusely.

Less than a month later, the same editor called me. "I had to fire Mel. He was so sarcastic the woman couldn't put up with him."

"I'm sorry—"

"I'm not blaming you," he said, "but please be careful about the people to whom you refer work."

I never heard from Mel again. And I felt guilty for not picking up on his sarcasm. That experience made me realize that the writers to whom I send work need to genuinely like other people and be able to get along with them.

• • •

Fourth, can you handle rejection? Here's another way to ask it: What if the author or the editor doesn't like your work?

This is a good question for anyone who wants to write for publication. But it's even more acute for collaborators. We have to please not only our clients, but the editors. Sometimes it's hard to satisfy both.

I've had a few experiences of being rejected by the author or the publisher. For example, about a year after I signed with my first agent, he set up a book deal for me. I flew to Denver and met with the man I'll call Dale, who had produced high returns when investing money for his clients.

Dale and I met for an exploratory meeting. I liked Dale, so I stayed over, and we started taping the material. He took me out for dinner that evening, and we talked about the publishing business and how a ghostwriter worked.

"One thing I can't do is work with someone who has to change every third word." I'd never said that before and don't know where it came from.

"No problem there," he said. "You're the expert with words; I'm the expert with numbers."

We did the taping, and I left. Dale asked if he could see the first two chapters before I went on with the book, and I agreed. As soon as I had completed two and polished them, I sent them to him.

A week later I had a special delivery from Dale. He had hacked up almost every sentence. Some of his corrections didn't make sense. I called Dale to see if we could work out our differences.

"I want to write a classic on investing. A classic. A book that will sell for at least twenty years, and you don't have the skills to write that."

Not only was that an awful rejection, but I felt I had failed. Maybe I was a terrible writer or just one who didn't know how to get into the heads of people who dealt with finances. (He must not have found a competent writer to produce a classic, because he never published.)

The second rejection came from a man who had been a cocaine addict, gotten clean, become a dynamic leader, and started a ministry on the West Coast to help addicts straighten out. A supporter of his ministry contacted me and agreed to pay me to write the man's story as a self-published book to use as a fundraiser.

She paid for my expenses to visit the former addict, and I had a marvelous time with him. He liked the first two or three chapters and showed them to a successful writer friend, who said they were good.

After I completed the entire manuscript, the author wrote back and said, "It's not dramatic enough. We're going to take the second half of your fee and give it to someone else who can add the elements we want."

Forget his ethics in doing that without asking the sponsor or talking to me. It was an absolute rejection. And it hurt, especially because I felt we had developed a relationship of trust.

A few months later he sent me a copy of the dramatic version. The new author used most of what I had written but inserted what I considered heavy-handed statements, often redundant. Regardless, the client hadn't liked my work and had rejected it. That's what I had to deal with.

The third painful rejection came from the publisher and not the writer. The author loved what I did, but the managing editor flew to Atlanta (where both of us lived) and said to me, "Yes, it's all right, but it needs—another layer of depth."

I had no idea what she meant, but she said they had hired another writer to add that power to the manuscript. When I received a copy of the book, nearly a year later, I understood what she meant by "another layer of depth." On page two of the book, I'd had the author saying, "I reached out for . . ." The new version said, "I ventured forth my hand . . ."

I guess I like being shallow.

As painful as it may be—and it's difficult—I read reviews on Amazon of books I've done. Now and then someone will say what a rotten book it was and that it was written by someone who was obviously an amateur.

Rejection comes in all forms, and to be successful, we have to keep at it, regardless.

• • •

If you become a ghostwriter fairly early in your career—that is, after you've developed the craft—collaborating can provide you with an opportunity to practice for the book you want to write or articles that burn in your heart. Your experience as a writer who produces and makes deadlines would certainly be a positive qualification if you want to write columns for a magazine or e-zine.

Ghostwriting offers a chance for you to learn how to write professionally, work with editors, and become familiar with the structure and formatting required. Best of all, you'll get paid, which is something you may not be able to achieve on your own for some time. Some things can only be learned by experience, so you can think of your time ghostwriting as part of your personal growth to improve your own writing skills.

Ghostwriting can also be preparation for work published under your own name, and it's an excellent way to network. While you're toiling away on a nonfiction piece for a small press or company, you inevitably come into contact with editors, publishers, and other professionals in the industry. The world of publishing is quite small, so you never know who you may meet. Do a good enough job ghostwriting that travel guide for your state, and you may land a job writing another piece for the same editor and get a byline with it.

Ghostwriting, like all professional writing, has three aspects: art, craft, and business. People who come to ghosts usually do so because they lack one or more of those necessary components. They don't know how to develop their ideas on paper (*art*). They don't know the *craft* involved in communicating with readers to keep them interested and committed to the book. They rarely know the publishing *business*.

Thus your task as the collaborator is to:

- Educate authors so they know what they're committing to do.
- Transform the manuscript, notes, or interviews into a marketable product.
- Maintain the voice so that the final product reads like the author and not the writer.

TAKEAWAYS

Here are questions to ask yourself if you want to move into ghostwriting as a career.

- Are you a self-starter? Are you self-disciplined? Can you meet deadlines?
- Can you treat collaboration as a business?
- Do you get along with people?
- Can you handle rejection?

10

WHAT ARE THE ADVANTAGES AND DISADVANTAGES OF GHOSTWRITING?

Let's start with the advantages of becoming a ghostwriter.

1. If you're successful, you'll be well paid. Many of those who engage your services are often prominent individuals and willing to pay enough to make sure the job is done well.

2. If you're talented, there's plenty of work available. Not only that, if you do a good job, the word spreads throughout the industry, and other editors seek your skills.

3. You may have the opportunity to work closely with prominent or famous individuals. Of course, not all your clients will be celebrities. Naturally, you also have the satisfaction of a job well done and the opportunity to continue to hone your writing skills. I value my relationships with the big names and have often learned a great deal being with them.

4. Most of the research comes from or through the subject. That makes the writing easier and quicker. The author can easily explain complicated concepts or help you grasp technical jargon. I've saved an immense amount of energy by asking, "And what does that term mean?" (Afterward, I go to the Internet to be sure their information is accurate.)

• • •

But along with the advantages, you need to be aware of the downside.

1. You receive no credit for your work. No matter how good your writing is, you usually can't take public credit for your ghostwritten pieces.

I recently read a post by an editor who said ghostwriters could not mention the name of their clients or books. Thirty years ago that was generally true. Today you can refer to those books and projects *unless specifically forbidden by the contract.*

2. Generally, your name isn't known, even if it's on the cover. I smile when people ask what I've written and I mention one or two big sellers and get the wide-eyed response, "You wrote that?"

Occasionally they get confused when I mention that I wrote *90 Minutes in Heaven* and ask, "What was it like going to heaven?"

My favorite experience took place in Detroit a decade ago. I was sitting next to two writers in a hotel, and our books were displayed on nearby tables. A woman walked up to the table and picked up *Gifted Hands*. "I read this book. It's a good one."

My friend Pam Perry said, "And here's the man who wrote it."

The woman stared at me. "You did not! Ben Carson wrote that book."

Pam picked up the book, pointed to my name, and said, "This is the man."

"Oh, all right." She dropped the book and walked away.

3. You receive no publicity, interviews, or talk shows. Some shy or introverted scribes consider that an advantage. But for most of us it's natural to want our names recognized for the work we've done.

You aren't able to publicly promote the book other than selling it when you speak. Don Piper has been incredibly generous to me and on several occasions asked me to join him at book signings. He's the only one who has ever done that. He puts out a monthly newsletter and often mentions something about me. And I appreciate his kindness.

4. Celebrities, even big-name leaders in religious circles, can be demanding and often don't realize it. The better known they are, the more they're protected by their own inner circle who tend to shield them and give them whatever they want.

My worst experience was with a famous public speaker. I lived in Atlanta, and he was in Southern California. The then-senior editor at Thomas Nelson had set up the agreement and said the man would be in touch with me. About a month later, I received a phone call from the author.

"There's a plane leaving Atlanta in three hours. Go to the Delta desk, and they'll have a ticket for you."

He was a bit brusque, but I did what he said. Someone met me when I arrived in Southern California. I had asked the man for four or five *full days* to get the information for a book about marriage, which was one of his areas of expertise.

In four days I had a total of less than five hours with him—he had too many appointments to rush to or details to take care of in his international ministry. I decided to go back to Atlanta the next day and told him so.

He was clearly unhappy and said, "If you stay one more day, I can give you an hour in the afternoon."

I tried to explain that this wouldn't be enough and that I needed to return home to work on my projects.

"You won't stay over for another hour tomorrow?"

I refused. I don't remember most of the conversation, but as I left him that day, I wanted to say to him, "Your life is obviously more important than mine, but I do have a life."

The publisher canceled the book, but not because of me. The author refused to write on the topic for which he had signed a contract.

5. Authors may demand endless rewrites. My worst experience was with a man who received the entire manuscript at once, which was the way he wanted it. When I do that, I ask authors to look it over and mark anything they don't like.

After I arrived at his office—at the time he set—he still kept me waiting more than hour. When his personal assistant brought me into his office, the author pulled out a hard copy of the manuscript and sat in one corner of the room. His assistant also had a printout and sat in the opposite corner. He placed me in the middle of the room with my laptop, facing both of them while he read aloud the entire manuscript, sentence by sentence. Sometimes he commented or objected to a word. His assistant also had a number of changes she thought I needed to make.

I didn't like it, but I remained as poised as I could and made every change they wanted. That took two days. Once home, I went over the entire manuscript and saw a few places where I could say things better to smooth out their revisions.

Two weeks later he asked me to return to his office, which I did. Again I waited for an hour (but I had anticipated that, so I worked on my laptop in his outer office).

The same experience again—sentence by sentence—and they had more changes. Few of them seemed significant; however, I made every change they wanted. That time he wanted to cut back on some of the self-revealing things that, in my opinion, made him more human.

"People may not understand," he said.

"They might respect you more if you tell," I said. When he insisted on cutting, I said, "I don't agree, but it's your book, and I do whatever you want."

He called me a third time (and paid my travel expenses each time). I'm not sure, but I think we reverted to some of the original language. But by then I didn't care. I just wanted to get the project done. The book did well, but I'm thankful he never asked me to write another one for him.

6. You have to earn the authors' trust and accept their suspicions about you and your motives. That aspect can be irritating, especially because you are a person of integrity.

Even though I don't like it, I don't fault people for being suspicious. When I wrote the autobiography of what I call a second-generation celebrity, he was clear about his mistrust.

"When I was a kid, so many people befriended me. But after a while they'd say, 'Can I meet your dad?' They didn't like me and only wanted to meet my father."

After we finished the book, he e-mailed and asked me to "return" all the cassette tapes from the interviews. "I used my own tapes," I said, "and I've already erased them."

He didn't respond.

When I wrote for a famous singer, I faced the same problem. I had to prove to him that he could trust me to be interested in him and his story and not want to sell him my own music. (I don't write music.)

7. Depending on your contract, you may have no editorial rights. That means you turn in the project and have absolutely no input after that. That one always rankled me. It happens less frequently than it did twenty years ago, and wise editors now send the edited pages to the collaborator. But when I did flat-fee projects, I worked hard to keep the author's intention, although a few times the editors distorted the meaning.

I'm not sure if the authors ever saw the completed manuscript, because after I turned in the manuscript and received the rest of my money, I had no further contact with the publishing house.

Here's one instance that upset me even though I had no way to appeal. One publisher decided to add thirty-two pages to make the book longer and to justify selling it for a higher price. They inserted pages from the author's journal without editing them. Perhaps I was prejudiced, but I felt pages of normal, daily activities did little for readers. For me, that intrusion took away any sense of pride of ownership I might have had with the book.

8. Your temperaments may not mesh. Most of us collaborators think we can work with anyone—until reality hits us. In 2004, I verbally agreed to write a book with two men—and the material was absolutely wonderful.

The second man, however, wasn't able to attend our initial get-acquainted meeting. The first author assured me that I would work well with his partner, whom I didn't meet until we started taping. The first three hours of the taping went well, but the partner was an extremely angry man.

Partner one was delightful, creative, and insightful. Whenever partner two spoke, I had to push away the anger and sarcasm behind his words and listen to what he meant.

That first day we had to stop early, so I left at noon. As soon as I was home, I called my agent and complained about the second partner. "I don't like him. He's angry, and even when he says something in a neutral voice, I sense he's ready to yell at me. I just don't want to work with him."

My agent understood and called them. Within an hour, partner two called me, enraged, and demanded that I honor my word and get back to work with them. I was a bit intimidated by his irate behavior, but I finally said, "It just won't work. My personality doesn't fit with yours. You need to get someone else."

The end of the story is that the first man eventually went on his own and wrote the book by himself (and I had told him he was capable), and it hit the *New York Times* best-seller list for a couple of weeks.

Therefore, I stress the importance of meeting *in person* before anything goes forward. One time my agent, Deidre Knight, and I talked about a book that was offered to me, but I didn't want to do it. "I can't explain why, only that I just don't want to do it."

"Listen to your instincts," Deidre said. "You don't have to provide an explanation. Just trust yourself."

That lesson enabled me to turn down several projects later on—and I can't give a reason for each, even afterward. But one sports figure in particular helped me get that message. I *knew* it wouldn't work. That's all I can say: I knew, although I couldn't explain it to anyone, let alone myself. I didn't do the book and have never regretted it.

TAKEAWAYS

The positive side of being a ghostwriter:
- The pay can be good.
- If you're talented, there is plenty of work available.
- You may have the opportunity to work closely with prominent or famous individuals.
- Most of the research comes from or through the subject.

Let's look at the disadvantages of becoming a ghostwriter:
- You receive no credit for your work.
- Generally, your name isn't known, even if it's on the cover.
- You receive no publicity, interviews, or talk shows.
- Celebrities—even Christians—can be demanding and often don't know it.
- Authors may demand endless rewrites.
- You have to earn authors' trust and accept their suspicions about you and your motives.
- You may have no editorial rights.
- Your temperaments might not mesh.

11

BREAKING INTO
GHOSTWRITING

The questions I hear most often from want-to-be collaborators is this: Where do I find clients? How do I let them know what I do? How do I get them to accept my fee and sign a contract?

The answers are simpler than you may think. Approach your self-marketing campaign step by step, the same way you'd approach writing a book.

What do you want to sell? This may seem obvious, but many writers have no idea what areas in which they want to work or what they have to offer. There are many ways to define yourself.

If asked today what I want to write for authors, I'd say, "I write books for underdogs who have achieved." One collaborator said, "I write articles and books for people with creative ideas."

That doesn't mean you're restricted to the way you define yourself, but it gives potential authors an idea of where your heart is. It's a way of saying, "I prefer to write on this—but I'm open to other ideas." My experience has been that authors who read and like one kind of book I've written usually have ideas for their own books that are similar.

After *90 Minutes in Heaven* came out, I received dozens of queries from people who had stories that involved dying or near-death experiences. I didn't say so, but I'd already written that book. I turned them down because I have a non-competitive clause in my contracts; however, I offered to give them the name of another ghostwriter.

If they said they wanted a name, I gave them only one because I didn't want them to audition writers. Then I added, "If this doesn't work out and you still want a reference, please contact me again." About one third of the time, they come back for a second reference, usually because the person to whom I sent them was unable to take on more projects at that time or wasn't interested in their material.

Even now when I offer a name, I also write in my e-mail, "I don't know her availability or her rates." I want to make certain they grasp that we writers don't work for free or purely on speculation.

I also try to be honest about whether I feel a royalty-paying publisher would be interested. Having one powerful life experience is marvelous, but I ask what they're doing *now*. "Publishers want people who are public speakers or have influence so they can sell their own books. Not only do you need to say that the event transformed your life, you have to show what you've done since then."

Sometimes I state that I write for royalty publishers and suggest, "If you want to consider self-publishing, I work with several writers whom I trust, and I'd be glad to refer them."

The above statement is especially important for me, as I want them to see that I have no personal or business interest in getting them to consider self-publishing.

Most ghostwriters who want to be successful in the field find ways to make it known that they have skills and are available for work. We're all different, but some collaborators suggest you approach people you think you'd like to write for and offer your services. I'd add, "Make sure your writing is good enough to publish. Get publishing experience first."

• • •

Here are my suggestions for breaking into the field.

1. Start with articles. I can't write that strongly enough. A book is a major undertaking that will require months, perhaps years. Recently I asked my agent how long the average author (her clients) needed to write a book.

"About seven months."

And they're professionals. They know how to write and what it involves. Your first book will take an enormous amount of time. But I also point out, "If you can write and sell articles, you can learn to do the same with books."

Think of an article as a miniature book with a hook— something to grab the reader—followed by the information or story you want to tell, and ending with a conclusion. Book structure is essentially the same.

2. Write profiles of individuals. They don't have to be famous, but look for people with unusual talents or achievements. Write their profiles for magazines and e-zines.

Let people know you're serious about being a collaborator. You might want to work for free to get experience. For example, I live in metro Atlanta, and a weekly newspaper is regularly thrown in my driveway. Each month I also pick up another free publication at the library or at local restaurants that covers our entire county. Bi-monthly in the mail, free and unsolicited, I receive something called *Up Close and Personal*. It's also devoted to this county and has a number of personal-experience articles. You can find individuals to write about, if you're willing to seek them.

To gain experience you might offer to work without pay. Perhaps you could contact some of those individuals or businesses and write for a magazine or an online organization that pays.

Check out blogs you like, especially those that give human-interest stories. Ask for the opportunity to write at no charge, of course, an article or a feature. Suggest the theme or person, and ask the blog owners if they're interested.

Some have suggested you approach high-profile individuals and ask to write a profile (and hope it will lead to a book). If you do, don't start with the top names. The bigger the name, the harder it will be to convince the person that they should hire you, especially if you're not experienced.

Perhaps focus on average people who do extraordinary things—what we call the human-interest story. The emphasis is on the event and not on the person. What about the boy who sold his toys to buy food for the hungry? The man who took homeless people into his house and helped them learn skills and start a new life? What about someone whose hobby is unusual?

How about a successful entrepreneur? Every Sunday the *Atlanta Journal-Constitution* has quite a nice interview with a successful business leader. If I were looking for work, there are several of them I'd follow through on.

Without being overbearing, let your friends know what you're doing. Tell your Sunday school class or your civic group. Talk to people at the gym. If you approach successful individuals, give them three or four ideas.

I'm not interested in following up on the people profiled in my Sunday paper, but sometimes for fun, as I read, I try to think of several ideas that I could pitch to them.

Many of these people overcame serious adversity, which the profile covers in one or two sentences. Serious illness set them backward, or bankruptcy nearly ruined them, or their business venture almost failed, so why did they hold on?

If you start with profiles and sell a few, you might discuss a book with the people you wrote about. You'll already have a wealth of information you can show publishers.

If you search for clients, be professional and look professional. Even though we live in a casually dressed world, unless you know it's all right, I wouldn't go in jeans or a pinstriped suit. Wear something that implies your professional level.

Point out to prospective clients the potential marketing benefits of a book. That way, even if your idea of a profile is essentially an ego trip for business entrepreneurs, you help them justify the costs. Make sure they understand that you will do all the writing and that nothing will appear in print without their approval.

3. Read newspapers and listen to the news, especially local news. Something that attracts national or international attention probably isn't worth trying to connect with. Publishers, agents, and other collaborators are already capitalizing on it.

For that reason I wouldn't go after guests on national talk shows. They often have books in the works (or already published). Watch for those whom others might overlook or not consider significant.

4. Gain professional experience as a writer in which you have to meet deadlines. I stress this because I think it's of vital importance. Editors like writers who establish a reputation of getting their work done on time. (My goal each time is to get a book to the publishing house before it's due.)

Even if you're a good writer, you need to make sure you complete the work according to the contract you signed and not just when you feel it's the best you can do. In fact, you need to combine the two.

5. Have a website. Get one immediately if you don't already have one. This is the most obvious way for you to advertise and sell yourself as a ghostwriter.

Be sure your site looks professional. Make it easy for prospective authors to try your services. List your publishing credits and pertinent life experiences. Offer the names of your satisfied clients (with their permission, of course).

If you haven't set up your website, Google topics such as "ghostwriting," and view their content. Type, "Where can I get free websites?" You'll find many groups such as WordPress or Wix.com. But check them out, because *free* may be only a come-on to get you to buy their expertise.

Scrutinize the way others have done their sites, and perhaps incorporate some of their ideas into your own. However, here are a few items you will certainly need:

- List the type of services you offer.
- Are you open to any kind of project? Would you consider erotica or books on gardening? Personal-experience stories? Business?
- Tout your experience and give authors reasons to hire you. It's like preparing a resume for a prospective employer (only not formal and boring). Anticipate their

questions, and give them basic information. Be as open as you can. Don't hold back, or your clients will sense it. Anticipate their questions, and provide answers to the burning issues they have such as their costs and the time it will take for you to do their books.

- Remind yourself that everything on your website speaks about you. I've read a few horrible ones—horrible because they misspell words or make grammatical mistakes. One woman referred to *divine* twice—and both times spelled it like the surname, Devine. That means you need someone to proof your site, no matter how carefully you've tried to make it right. Before you read this book, at least two people will have gone over it to check for misspellings and errors.

6. Make sure you have business cards. This isn't an option. If you can't afford a creative business card, there are any number of companies that will print them cheaply. Check the Web. The best-known company is Vistaprint, which I've used.[7]

Always carry business cards with you. Always. When you speak with anyone socially, have cards ready. Don't hand them out indiscriminately, but be ready to hand one out if a person shows interest in your ghostwriting or says, "I know someone who might be interested."

Make sure your card has your contact information, especially your e-mail. When people contact me, I try to acknowledge every potential client within twenty-four hours—which also shows my professionalism. I respond with a short paragraph to make it clear whether I'm interested.

After my first batch of printed cards ran out, I deleted my telephone number—for self-protection. Why no phone

7   http://www.vistaprint.com/business-cards.

number? Because prospects will call. In the beginning that may not be a problem, but some people want to talk endlessly.

Here's my maxim: those who have the least to say take the longest to say it.

You can handle e-mails at *your* convenience. Also, forcing them to write what they want enables you to have some sense of whether it's of interest to you.

I used to get calls from people with a pitch that went something like this: "I have a great idea—something no one has ever thought of before. If you'll write it, we'll both make a million dollars." Need I comment on that?

Another problem from prospective clients is that many of them have no money or don't realize that it will cost them. Because I work primarily within the Christian writing field, occasionally I receive telephone queries saying, "God gave you a gift, so . . ." They go on to quote Bible verses about giving freely and using our gifts for others.

"I don't work for nothing," I responded. "It's my gift, but it's how I make a living. Does your Christian dentist give you free service?"

7. Consider printed brochures. I've never used them because I've been fortunate in that clients seek me. But if you want to let people know about your services, I suggest you create a simple but tasteful threefold brochure. On quality paper, nicely design a piece that spells out who you are and what you offer.

Try to show how you're different from others with similar services. You might be faster or provide extra options such as helping authors find a publisher.

The brochures don't have to be elaborate or expensive. In the summer of 2014, I spoke at a writers conference in Cedar

Falls, Iowa. One of the conferees handed me a brochure for his ghostwriting services. It was his first one, and I think it will get better as he goes along. The inside of the threefold brochure was titled "Package Options," and he listed them as silver, gold, platinum, and diamond. I liked the up front approach.

8. You need a blog. Do you blog? The correct answer is, "Yes, I blog regularly." If you don't already, start *today*. Think of the topics dearest to your heart, and write about them, at least once a week. A few ambitious types do it daily, but most can't keep to that schedule.

I have two twice-weekly blogs. I knew that if I tried to write for two blogs every week, I'd never remain faithful. By writing enough posts for eight or nine weeks at a time, it's easier for me to commit. When I'm overwhelmed with other projects, as I was while working on this book, I did a series of encores on my blogs. That is, I reprinted material from four or five years ago. My experience says that most people don't go into the archives, and if enough time has lapsed, your followers probably won't remember.

9. Don't overlook social-media sites. Most writers feel their presence is mandatory on Twitter, Facebook, Pinterest, LinkedIn, and other sites. I have several social media accounts, but I'm not personally involved. The woman I hire to facilitate my sites, creates graphics and posts snippets from things I've written. She keeps me informed of special comments and lets me know if questions come in that she can't answer.

You'll have to figure out for yourself how involved you want to become in social media.

Some former addicts have told me that they rely on things like setting a timer or the clock on their smartphones. They might allow themselves thirty minutes each day and then stop.

10. Enlist your own connections. Don't overlook your friends and business associates. Once you start ghostwriting, the best advertisement I know is the satisfied customer.

For example, although I never asked, Stan Cottrell referred me to others, and one of them was Norman Vaughan. Until his death in 2005, Norm was the last surviving member of the historic group that went to Antarctica in 1928, when Admiral Richard Byrd made his historic flight over the South Pole.

Because of Stan, Norman contacted me, and we wrote two books together. The first, *With Byrd at the Bottom of the World*, came out in 1990, and is still in print. Other satisfied authors, like Ben Carson, sent people my way, and I published at least six books because of his personal recommendations.

11. Post information about your services on writing forums. Two collaborators have suggested Craigslist. Three writers mentioned local newspapers.

Every Wednesday Angela Hoy's WritersWeekly.com newsletter comes out, and it's worth looking at. Hoy's website and newsletter provide expert advice, success stories, and listings for paying writing markets and freelance jobs.

12. Consider writing family histories. This is a lucrative field, even if its purpose is only to leave a written legacy to a person's grandchildren. Two members of the church I attend self-published ghostwritten books. Both authors are in their nineties now, and it's a wonderful time in their lives for them to record their experiences in World War II.

Tell prospects they need to tell their story before it's too late. Not many people may want to read these stories, but certainly family members and members of the same organizations would.

Check out organizations devoted to seniors. Offer to speak to them and explain what you do.

13. Join organizations and attend writers conferences. Don't join only to hunt for prospects, but select those in which you have an interest. American Business Women or Toastmasters would seem obvious. Quite likely you'll meet people with excellent personal experience stories or ideas.

Attend writers conferences with a sincere desire to learn and grow. Don't push yourself. Meet people naturally.

I shouldn't need to say that, but I've met many conferees who spend most of their time running around, trying to push or sell themselves to others. Too often I've encountered the desperate types who constantly jump on anyone they think might help them.

I met one of my customers at a conference, and here's something he said to me: "I like you because you didn't want anything from me." He said, "You were open, and I didn't sense you were pushing anything."

14. Should you pay for ads? You can buy advertising, and many do, but be careful. It's expensive, particularly when you first start. The lack of response is the biggest complaint I've heard.

One writer appeared on a national TV show, and in the conversation he mentioned that he was open to do more ghostwriting. They placed his telephone number and website on the bottom of the screen. Although he didn't pay for it, it was still an ad; he didn't receive a single query, which discouraged him.

Some pay for tiny ads in the backs of magazines, but I question the wisdom of that. People might go there to look for a ghostwriter, but why would they?

One magazine editor told me that an ad has to appear at least three months in a row before most advertisers see results. I don't know if that's normal, but it says it's costly to advertise.

If you have a narrow field such as family histories, choose a specific market in which to advertise. That's probably a wiser investment. My suggestion: don't buy advertising unless you can afford to spend the money without receiving results.

15. Help others. It's sad but vastly overlooked, even in our Christian culture. Jesus said, "So in everything, do to others what you would have them do to you."[8] He also said, "Give, and it will be given to you. A good measure, pressed down, shaken together and running over, will be poured into your lap. For with the measure you use, it will be measured to you."[9]

Because I try to live that way, one of my earliest commitments in writing was to help others any way I could. A few times I've turned down good projects because I knew someone else whom I thought could do a better job.

That may seem a rather oblique way to operate, but I've repeatedly proven in my own life the cliché that says "What goes around comes around."

Every major step I've made in my career has been because someone else took the initiative. I haven't looked for or depended on it, but in retrospect I see it plainly.

After I had sold at least one hundred articles, I wasn't thinking about a book. However, my wife and I had spent a great deal of time with a professional writer, Charlotte, who was going through a divorce. We wanted to help her, and we expected nothing in return.

One day Dr. Ben Campbell Johnson, who was then a publisher, called and asked me to write a book for his house. "Charlotte said good things about you and showed me some of your articles. I like the way you write."

8   Matthew 7:12.
9   Luke 6:38.

"I've never written a book," I said.

"Yes, I know," he said. "Tell me what you're working on these days."

During the conversation I mentioned that because I was a pastor I did the research for my sermons and then added some of my own ideas to write the articles.

"I'm preaching and writing a series on prayer." As the words popped out, I realized that this was probably the most over-written topic in religious writing.

"Tell me about one of your ideas." After I did Ben said, "I like that. Nice angle. Tell me another."

After giving me four or five thumbs up, he said, "Could you write thirty chapters on prayer?"

By then I had recovered enough to say, "Yes, I can do that." (I already had twelve articles written.)

We called the book *Prayer: Pitfalls and Possibilities*. It didn't sell well, probably less than two thousand copies, but it was my start.

Then I met Ross Cockrell, who was in charge of sales for the publishing house. Six months later Ross went to work for my denominational publishing house.

Within a month Dick Ray, the senior book editor, called. "Ross has told me about your writing. I'd like you to consider writing for us."

I did two books for that publishing house.

In my first draft of this book, I cited eight career examples (though I've cut it down to four) that came about because I went out of my way to help someone else. I stress this because my personal experiences show how God has honored my fol-lowing the golden rule in Scripture. I'm amazed, however, at how seldom people seem to listen to my advice.

Takeaways

How do you break into the field of ghostwriting?

- Start with articles.
- Write profiles.
- Read newspapers and listen to the news, especially local news.
- Gain professional experience as a writer where you have to meet deadlines.
- Have a website.
- Make sure you have business cards.
- Consider using printed brochures.
- Start your own blog.
- Don't overlook social media sites.
- Enlist your friends and other connections.
- Post information about your services on writing forums.
- Consider writing family histories.
- Join organizations and attend writers conferences.
- Should you buy ads? You can buy advertising and many do, but be careful.
- Remember the golden rule: help others.

12

SHOULD YOU SPECIALIZE
OR GENERALIZE?

In your first forays into collaborative writing—unless you're sure you know the area in which you want to specialize—I suggest you open yourself to any offers that come your way. Try various genres. Learn what you can do and what you don't do well or takes too much energy out of you. In doing so, you may discover strengths (or weaknesses) of which you weren't aware.

In the beginning most of us successful ghostwriters were generalists. We tried to write on any subject. That's an easy way to begin, as most of us said yes to anything we thought would sell. As we grew in experience, we realized our limitations and interests.

I want to note that during the first years of their careers, most writers don't know what will sell. If the topic interests them and they write the book well enough, they assume a publishing house will buy it.

Wisdom or understanding usually comes through sad experiences. In my early days I took on several projects because individuals came to me, told me their story, and added, "All my friends (everyone/my writers group/my Sunday school class/my college professors/my dentist) tell me I need to have a book." Or they move into public speaking, and afterward several people say, "You need to put that into a book."

Because of my naïveté in the publishing field, I agreed to work on several projects that didn't sell. During the first three or four years, I was so eager to write more collaborations (and most of them were personal experiences) that I didn't charge to write the first two chapters. Because I began my career before the advent of the book proposal, a few times I wrote the entire manuscript only to have publishers turn them down.

In those days we sent a hard copy to a publisher and waited for a response before trying another publishing house. If our manuscript was rejected, we retyped the soiled pages and sent the entire book to another publisher. Sometimes it took two years to get three rejections.

The point is that I often had no idea what sold and what didn't (you may not either), even though I had already published a handful of books of my own plus those sent to me by an editor.

Some things we learn by doing and failing. At least it was true with me. Slowly I grasped what would or would not sell. In 1990, eight years into my ghostwriting career, Christian publishers started turning to literary agents. That's when I first learned of book proposals.

The advent of agents certainly speeded up the process. They could, and did, send proposals to several editors—and in those days through the postal service. They knew the editors and likely had dealt with them before, which gave them an edge.

At least they received responses faster than unknown writers.

For me, among many, many good reasons for having an agent, the most important was to get a response to a book idea before I wrote anything. Even today, twenty years later, I usually e-mail Deidre Knight a paragraph or two of what I have in mind and ask for her opinion. She has a sharp business sense about whether she can sell the ideas.

agent

• • •

If you continue to collaborate, you'll figure out the areas where you do your best work. You'll become more (or less) enthusiastic about certain types of material.

Here's something else I do. I tell my best friend, David Morgan, about an idea without censoring myself. He listens carefully until I finish and picks up clues of which I'm not aware.

"Your voice shows your enthusiasm for this project," he might say. Or, "You're telling me it sounds like a good project, but you don't seem to feel that way."

I also pray about a project every day until I have a sense of whether to accept or turn it down. In early 2014, a man in the Detroit area told me a powerful story of how he had escaped death by an intruder, which led him into a significant, viable inner-city ministry. He fascinated me, and I almost said yes on the spot.

Eventually I turned him down (and offered to refer him to another writer). I have no objective reason for my decision. I prayed and waited for some kind of answer. Although I believe God does speak, I don't want to blame the Holy Spirit if I'm wrong. So I refer to this process as listening to my intuitive voice. And when that intuitive voice "hears," I obey whatever answer I receive.

• • •

I learned to specialize. In chapter 11, I said I'm especially drawn to underdogs, or invulnerables, a term coined in the late 1980s—those who overcome nature and achieve without nurturing or encouragement.

When I wrote my second book for Dr. Ben Carson, *Think Big*, I knew that was my area. Ben was an invulnerable, and his was probably the most amazing story I've ever written about someone from an inauspicious beginning who achieved worldwide fame.

Looking at my resume, I've produced quite a spectrum of books, but when asked, "What's your favorite?" I go back to people like Ben Carson, Stan Cottrell, John Turnipseed, and Katariina Rosenblatt. There are others, like Don Piper, but the first four stand out because they developed successful careers in spite of overwhelming odds.

While working with them, I grasped what made them hold on when they should have failed. And that taught me to see myself clearly.

I like to think of it this way: most of us gravitate toward books, films, or anything else with the same recurring themes we have in our own lives. Without going into a lengthy history, I came from a family in which my dad and his father were alcoholics, and my three brothers followed the pattern. Dad often beat me during my childhood, and I was sexually assaulted by others several times before the age of eight. So naturally I was moved by stories of overcomers and high achievers.

I also believe that most of us writers have perhaps half a dozen emotional issues in our lives—areas we haven't resolved. We're touched by those topics and gravitate toward them without consciously understanding the reason.

For example, I can point to two famous female novelists whose settings are always among the wealthy and beautiful. One of them came from an impoverished British background, so the reason seems fairly obvious. I don't know about the other, but her books seem almost obsessed with riches. I'm not criticizing, only pointing out that they're probably writing from their life themes.

The classic example for me is Charles Dickens. Most people know of his sad childhood, which is reflected in many of his novels—*Oliver Twist, David Copperfield, Great Expectations*, and *A Christmas Carol*.

Here's a lesson I learned long ago, and it comes from my experience and commitment as a collaborator: everything we say and do gives hints of who we are. We unfold and announce ourselves through our writing.

I smile when I remember the remarks of Twila Belk, my virtual office assistant. She began working for me in 2007, and often commented on little aphorisms and maxims I wrote, especially in my newsletters.

Here are two examples:

I'm passionately involved in the process; I'm emotionally detached from the result.

The messes in life are my best teachers; I don't like them, but I need them.

After two years Twila said to me, "Those insights are really about you. Did you know that?"

I did know and smiled because she had caught on.

I can somewhat monitor my spiritual and emotional growth by reflecting on some of those pieces. When collaborating, no matter how hard I work to sound like the author, my own values sneak through. That's not an apology, only reality. I don't think my values detract from my writing, because they also reflect the person with whom I work.

• • •

This leads to my next point: *Pass up work that you can't do well.* This is important, even though you may have trouble admitting that someone else can do a better job on a particular book than you could.

At the time of this writing, I've done four books with Don Piper, a man I love and respect. He came to me with a fifth book that he wanted to write himself—and it was something extremely close to his heart. He asked me to function primarily as a book doctor.

I told Don no and sent him to my good friend Larry Leech, whom I knew could do a good job. My reason is that I'm more of an intuitive writer, or to use the language of some, a right-brainer. Like anyone else, I can *function* from the logical, analytical left-brain side, but it's what I call my inferior mode.

Months later Don said it was going well and he liked Larry's work. That was a good move for all three of us. Don received the help he needed; Larry took on a new project to stretch himself; and I didn't have to torture myself by working in my inferior mode.

I work with a cadre of writers to whom I send work that, even if I think it's top quality, I know they could do a better job on than I could. In writing this, I also say that it took me a few years to admit that. In the early days, I was positive I could write on any topic. Perhaps that's true, but when I think of the *quality of work*, I joyfully admit that sometimes I defer to others.

• • •

What kind of ghostwriter are you? What's your specialty? You may not know, and that's all right. Experience will teach you, and at some point in your career, it will be of invaluable help for you to know when a want-to-be author first contacts you.

Every good ghostwriter has a specialty. It may be business, education, or health and fitness. For example, I consider Sally Jenkins, whom I mentioned in chapter 5, the best collaborator in her field—which is sports.

What do you care about? What excites you? What do you dislike?

Focus on those things about which you are already passionate or can become enthusiastic. Never write only for the money. Seek work, but pass up projects you're not interested in doing.

When you meet prospective authors, trust your instincts. If you don't get a good feeling about who they are within the first few minutes of the meeting, you probably aren't going to make a successful ghostwriter for that person. One of the qualities of a good ghost is the ability to intuit. You may not always be accurate on the interpretation of your feelings, but you will know when something inside you whispers no.

TAKEAWAYS

- Remain open to any idea or book project.
- To specialize or generalize is a serious question until you know exactly what areas in which you want to write.
- Some lessons you can learn only by experience or by failing.
- Recruit someone who knows you and can help you discern if a project is for you.
- Discover *your* life themes, which will help you figure out the areas in which you write best.
- Pass up work that you can't do well, and refer the authors to writers who can do it better.

13

YOU NEED TO DEVELOP
TRUST

Even though true, it's too simplistic to say, "The ability to be a ghostwriter is a gift." After I had collaborated on at least twenty books, I finally accepted that I had a gift. And I want to make it clear, it's not the essential requirement.

For many projects, anyone who can write well can become a ghostwriter. Immediately I think of the objective, informational book or article. The personality isn't significant; people want the content. So if you can write with a clear, logical flow, you could certainly do certain types of collaborating.

Yet when it comes to writing that is identified with a person, you need specific qualities to do a good job.

First, you have to get inside the heart of the author. When I began my career as a ghostwriter, it was because one editor, Victor Oliver, told me, "You know how to get inside the heads of other people." I've pondered his words off and on since then. His statement *summed up* the result of what a reliable ghostwriter accomplishes—you get inside and open up the heart of the author.

Second, I want to point out that my list of needed qualities for a ghostwriter is my own and have come about by reflecting on the success of my work. But at the top of the list is this: your author must trust you, and developing that conviction is your responsibility. The author may hire you for a variety of reasons, but you need to *earn* your client's confidence.

That means that the individuals with whom I work must be assured that I'm reliable and dependable and will guard their secrets. Especially that last item—guard their secrets.

Too many people have been entrusted with privileged information and later have written or tried to publish a tell-all book. Paul Burrel, once butler to the late Princess Diana, wrote a tell-everything book that was an international best seller. He broke no laws, but I find that kind of book contemptible. He was in a position of trust and revealed those matters even though Princess Diana was no longer alive.

Twice in my career I've been approached by ex-wives of celebrities to tell "the real story," and I've turned them down. To me, it comes under the category of propriety and honor.

One thing celebrities learn quickly is that people find great pleasure in revealing the stars' secrets. Perhaps it makes them feel more important or they think it puts them into a special class. Or they believe they become important by being associated with the powerful.

Regardless of the reason, the famous people I've worked with have been naturally cautious. I've had to present myself in such a way that they dropped their guard and trusted me. The sooner we establish a trusting bond, the stronger the relationship and the better our finished product.

• • •

Perhaps if I were more insightful, I could explain how to foster the confidence the author has in me, but I can't. However, I've realized two things: First, nothing significant happens unless the authors are convinced that I won't betray their secrets. Second, I sense when trust is present. Maybe not the exact moment, but something mystical happens when the authors let down their guard and rely on me.

When that happens—and I can't think of a single book I've published where it wasn't there—I feel an energy, a kind of empowering. Most of all, there's a deep rapport—an intimacy. They don't hold back.

The authors need to feel that way. Whether they're conscious of their vulnerability in my presence is not clear. The most revealing action is when they cry. It happens because they have the permission and the freedom to dive deeply into themselves and reach places they haven't touched before.

• • •

My first realization of deep trust came when I wrote my second collaboration, *No Mountain Too High*, with Stanley Cottrell Jr. (He's given me permission to write this.)

One day Stan was telling about his childhood, and that, although the oldest of six siblings, he was short—about half a foot shorter than his six foot two father. Apparently Stanley Sr. detested the boy's small stature and never seemed to let him forget he was undersized.

While we were taping, Stan started to relate instances of severe beatings he had endured as a child. Before he'd said more than a dozen sentences, he burst into tears. He shocked me as he described those beatings.

Thirty years later Stan and I saw the film *Twelve Years a Slave* together. Afterward he said, "That beating scene of the black woman near the end was hard to take." He went on to say that it reminded him of his childhood.

In 1982, I hadn't been able to handle everything Stan told me. My father used to beat me, but I wasn't ready to deal with my own issues. I point this out because this is a significant factor in writing personal experience stories: *sometimes the writers can't handle the authors' self-revelations.*

Above I wrote, "I hadn't been able to handle," but I wasn't conscious of that inability. I listened and waited silently until Stan stopped crying before we moved on. Only later did I recognize my discomfort.

Because I didn't have editorial rights, what I'd call an old-school editor deleted the little I wrote about this. He didn't like seriously unpleasant things in books.

Even so, at least twice during the years that followed, Stan referred to that crying incident. He readily admits that when we were working on the book was the first time he had faced the pain of the beatings.

Stan, as a runner, has now run more than two hundred thousand miles—as far I can tell, the most recorded of any living runner. At various times he's established records for the fastest run from New York to San Francisco, the most miles run in twenty-four hours, and he was the first Westerner to run two thousand four hundred miles along the Great Wall of China. A year before we met, Stan had completed a run across thirteen countries in Europe in fifty-eight days.

His secret: he doesn't feel physical pain like normal people do. That's what the frequent and severe beatings did to him.

By contrast, thirty years later I wrote the autobiography of Katariina Rosenblatt titled *Stolen: The True Story of a Sex Trafficking Survivor*. As she described her childhood abuse that made her susceptible to traffickers, I was able to listen without flinching. In fact, in the opening chapter, using Kat's voice, I described that our childhoods had many similarities. The difference was that I wasn't lured into sex trafficking even though my background would have made me a good victim.

TAKEAWAYS

- Nothing truly significant or effective will happen unless authors trust you and are convinced you won't betray their secrets.
- You can sense when trust is present because the authors don't hold back.
- To be fully effective, you need to be able to handle any negative, unpleasant revelations from the author.

14

WHAT MAKES A GOOD
GHOSTWRITING PROJECT?

When someone asks me how I choose a good ghostwriting project, the final answer comes down to this: I have to feel a strong, positive response to the person and the project.

It's difficult to explain, so I'll tell you my method and then quote other collaborators who share their different approaches.

- If the concept doesn't grab my interest, I decline.
- If I am interested, I find out enough to sense whether it will be a good fit for me and if I think we can sell it to a publisher.
- My next step is to insist on a face-to-face meeting. It's sometimes expensive for the person to come to me or pay my expenses to visit. But it's vital.
- When I meet with individuals, I get caught up in their story. Recently I learned the word that describes me: *empath*. If this is also new to you, my dictionary says an empath is one who is able to tune in to the emotional experience of a person.

- I have to get away from the individual's influence. If I make a decision while I'm with them, it's because of their empathic impact. Only after I'm physically away am I able to listen *objectively* to what I call my inner wisdom.

As previously stated, I frequently receive e-mails. Some from others for whom I've written, some by referral, and a few from people who search the Internet for ghostwriters and find my name. Regardless of the source, I need that inner sense that it's for me before I say yes.

Occasionally I'll be uncertain, and that's when I ask others, especially my agent, for input.

• • •

I contacted several collaborators and asked what attracted them to a project. Here are their responses.

"I look at two things," Larry Leech wrote. "The first is the person and their motive. I've encountered people who want a book to launch them into the stratosphere or resurrect a once-flourishing career. The ones who have this second mind-set are usually the toughest to work with. In their desperation they often suck the life out of the project.[10]

"Second, I have yet to run across someone who *doesn't* feel they have some kind of story. So I look at the topic itself. How can we take that person's topic/idea and write it in a way that will interest readers?"

Kathy Bruins adds, "I've found that it's having good communication where both parties are in sync with one another. They understand what I'm saying without a lot of

---

10   Larry Leech, lleech@cf.rr.com.

explanation and what I'm thinking without my having to say all the words, and vice versa.[11]

"Both parties also have similar goals for the project and aren't afraid to challenge the other one when they feel a change is needed, and the recipient of the challenge is not defensive but appreciates the input."

From James Pence comes this advice by asking questions:

First, is the project viable? To answer this question, I consider two other questions. Is there a reasonable possibility that a publisher might be interested in the project? If not, then, if the idea is unlikely to find a publisher, does the author want to self-publish, and does he/she have the financial resources to pay me to write the book?

If I decide that the project is viable, then I ask, "Does the project or story intrigue me?" If I don't find the project/story interesting, I'm not likely to take it on.

Is the client/author someone I feel I can work with? It's hard to be certain of this with only a few conversations to go on, but it's still a consideration.

I don't ghost or collaborate on fiction. I've done it twice so far and have not been pleased with the process either time. For me, writing fiction is a personal journey of discovery, and it's difficult for me to share this process with others."[12]

---

11   Kathy Bruins, kbruins77@gmail.com.

12   James Pence, jamespence919@gmail.com.

Jeanne Marie Leach answered the question this way: "If someone wants a ghostwriter to write a mystery or a suspense novel or a book on how to change a car engine, I'm out. But if it's an adventure or a memoir, I'll consider it."[13]

"I've done one ghostwriting book, which was referred to me through a publishing company I was already doing some contract work for," Donna Schlachter wrote. "I've also written two work-for-hire books that came from meeting the book compiler at a writers conference.[14]

"In each case, I considered the topic, the specifications, the turnaround time, and the money offered. Then my husband and I both prayed about it, read the contract, and determined what we thought we could bring to the project.

"Each time, there was more work than we'd anticipated, but I found the projects rewarding and would do it again."

Peggy Matthews Rose stated simply that she and the author need a shared worldview and passion for the topic. "I was recruited to coauthor a book in 2002," she said. "His topic, but I wrote it all and was listed as the 'and' author on the cover. Went on to do five more with him. Also I networked with folks at my church who needed writing collaboration."[15]

Margot Starbuck wrote,

> I got my first ghostwriting gig through my agent. I would never have known that I possessed that skill if he'd not had the confidence in my writing to recommend me. The next few gigs were also through the same agency—me saying

---

13   Jeanne Marie Leach, jlmtnlady@colorado.net.

14   Donna Schlachter, Donna@livebytheword.com.

15   Peggy Matthews Rose, pegrose@mac.com.

yes and hoping I could deliver. (Great news: I could.)

At writing conferences I let editors know I was doing editing, collaborating, and ghostwriting. When they said they were including me in their "file," I naturally assumed that file was code for trash can. But one day an editor at a major publisher contacted me because she thought I'd be perfect for their client.

So my experience has been that ghostwriting is definitely a slow-build endeavor. The best fit is when I'm passionate about the material the subject is sharing. For example, I never would have dreamed of writing for an international non-profit organization, about a woman born in Uganda and released from poverty through child sponsorship, who is now encouraging North American families to live as God's agents in the world. . . .

Projects that aren't good fits have been those where I feel frustrated by a client who doesn't communicate clearly (which, of course, is why I got the job) or if it's a bad match theologically.[16]

• • •

I've presented these responses to help you as a prospective collaborator learn how we ghostwriters decide on whether to accept a project. As you've seen, there are no six steps, and each of us handles the question differently.

---

16   Margot Starbuck, margotstarbuck@gmail.com.

TAKEAWAYS

My way to choose a project:
- If the concept doesn't grab my interest, I decline.
- If I am interested, I find out enough to sense whether it will be a good fit for me and can sell it to a publisher.
- I insist on a face-to-face meeting.
- When I meet with individuals, I get caught up in their story. The word that describes me is empath—one who is able to tune in to the emotional experience of a person.
- I have to get away from the individual's influence. Only after I'm physically away am I able to listen objectively to what I call my inner wisdom.

Consider the responses from established collaborators on what makes a good writing project:
- Try to discern the person's purpose in writing.
- Make sure you're in sync with communication and have similar goals.
- Decide if the project is for a royalty publisher. If not, does the author want to self-publish, and if so, does the author have the finances to pay the fees?
- Consider specifications such as turnaround time and money.
- Both the author and the writer need a passion for the topic.

15

WHAT DO YOU WANT FROM AUTHORS?

If you let authors know what you expect from them, you'll both have a smoother relationship. For example, ask how available they are and the best way for you to communicate with them. Some may want text messages, others e-mails or phone calls.

It's especially important to tell them how much time you'll need to interview them. This means you'll first have to figure out how much time *you* need for the interviewing process.

For the first eight or nine years of my collaborating, I asked for five full days. I was still learning how to function in my role. Then I dropped a day from my requirement. Because of my long experience, I've learned shortcuts to get the information and now ask for only two full days (and that includes all day and evening).

One reason I can keep it short is that I find out everything I can about the author before we do our initial work together. If they're already public figures, I ask them to send me copies of the articles or profiles on them that they liked best. Those favored pieces say that the author believes the writers under-stood. Franklin Graham told me that an article in *Gentlemen's Quarterly* was the best he'd read, and Ben Carson picked a Sunday-edition article from the *Detroit Free Press*.

• • •

You also need to explain to your authors how you work and how you will respond. By this I mean that after I've taped material, I can say, "Within four weeks I'll have a rough draft of the first three chapters for you."

Then I ask them how long it will take for them to respond to me. That's important, because if the book is a significant project, you need a timely response. Sometimes I'll say, "Will it be possible for you to have this back to me within a week?"

By giving authors a deadline, I remain in control of the process and also let them know and accept their responsibility. If they say a week isn't enough time, we negotiate.

For instance, after I finish an outline (which I don't show them), I write the first two or three chapters. My first attempt is to catch their voice. When I send the writing, I explain that it's a rough draft and ask the authors to make changes to any mis-conceptions. I also tell them the material hasn't been proofed and will likely contain typos that my eyes didn't catch.

I ask them to write any comments right in the manuscript in **bold** so I won't miss them.

Once they've returned those early chapters, I polish them and add what I call the Technicolor process. I smooth out sen-tences and add details that readers might want to know.

• • •

Another thing is to make it clear to authors how you will communicate and how often. You might check in with them every week, show them each completed chapter, or hibernate in your office until you're finished. They need to know what to expect from you.

My general experience is that authors like to see the first few chapters ASAP. Because I work with a literary agent and write proposals for my collaborative projects, that means I have to write an overview of the book and sample chapters. As soon as I've refined those early chapters with the author's corrections, the full proposal goes to my agent. She makes out her hit list and e-mails the proposals to prospective editors.

Once we've sold the book, I prefer to finish the manuscript and send it as a whole so the author can see the connections. Although when some authors are too anxious to wait, I send each piece as I complete it. I try to avoid this approach, because authors will sometimes want to insert information that I believe should come in later. Most of the time, they agree to wait.

I prefer they not show any part of the manuscript to their friends until we have the finished product. I say *prefer* because most of my first-time clients are so excited and enthusiastic that they share it with a number of people, which embarrasses me because it's not a perfect manuscript.

• • •

When you work with clients, you also need to explain the writing process and get their cooperation. Give them approximate timelines for each step in the process.

Finally, be clear about the grammar and writing style. It may not be necessary in most cases, but sometimes you encounter a client who thinks she knows grammar but really doesn't. Or punctuation. Explain that the content of the book is totally theirs; the style and grammar are yours. (If you take that position, be sure you really know grammar—not all ghosts do.)

TAKEAWAYS

You need to make authors aware of what you need from them and what you will provide:

- How long you require to interview them.
- How long they will wait from the time of the taping until you have something to show them.
- How soon you expect them to return the corrected manuscript.
- The content is theirs; the grammar and writing style are yours.

16

YOU CAN GIVE IDEAS
TO AUTHORS

Imagine the following conversation.

"I think you need to write a book," you say to the highly successful executive. "I'm a ghostwriter, and I'd like to write it for you."

"I like the idea, but what would I write about?" the CEO asks. "I don't want to tell my personal story—too many of those are out there, and mine isn't that unusual. Besides, I don't have any good ideas."

"I've been thinking about that," you say, "and I have three ideas for you to consider."

Because you did your research before meeting with the CEO, you're not merely throwing out the first thoughts that come to you. You prepared for the meeting, and the three suggestions (or perhaps five) express your seriousness.

The above illustration is to show that you can give ideas to potential clients. What you offer may be extremely obvious to you but not to them. Your suggestions haven't occurred to them, because they're part of the CEO's work and lifestyle.

• • •

How do you prepare to offer ideas?

Let's not deal with an autobiography as a possibility, although that may work. Do some serious research about the prospect. Learn as much as you can. If she's a public figure— even if not famous—you can probably find a lot of background information. As I pointed out previously, each Sunday the *Atlanta Journal-Constitution* does a profile of successful CEOs. Suppose you chose one of them.

After you read the brief profile, you agree that the person's success is impressive, but you say, "I don't have any good ideas to present to her."

When I work with someone who wants to do more than one book, I suggest they start with their story—which is what people want to read. Their story becomes part of their credentials for writing the next. You suggest that the book that follows be one of her innovative ideas or principles.

Here's an example of what I mean. Before *Gifted Hands* came out, Ben Carson had already performed surgeries that brought him prominence, especially when he and a team from Johns Hopkins separated conjoined twins who shared arteries and veins. It was a breakthrough surgery.

Although he received a lot of publicity, that single surgery didn't make him an international figure; it did help establish his credentials. When the publisher contacted me to write his story, I agreed.

His story, in my mind, was more important. However, Ben has long used an acrostic he calls T H I N K B I G. I thought the concept was excellent and should be a separate book. The first book would introduce Ben's remarkable rise from being known as a dummy in school to his outstanding work as a pediatric neurosurgeon. The second book, I said, would expound on his principles.

The editor overruled and said, "No, we want you to include the principles at the end of the book."

We did, and *Gifted Hands* became a phenomenal success. A year later, the editor called me. "We'd like you and Ben to do a follow-up book called *Think Big*."

Even though I pointed out that we had already included that topic and devoted the last chapters of the book to it, she said they wanted us to make it into a motivational book.

Careful not to include material from the acrostic in *Gifted Hands*, Ben and I wrote *Think Big*, which has done extremely well. Published in 1992, it has never been out of print.

From a personal perspective, I believe I was correct in wanting to withhold the acrostic for two reasons. First, *Gifted Hands* was Ben's autobiography. Including the acrostic departed from that single purpose. Second, I felt the first book would prepare readers to want to see a second book, maybe more.

That experience helped me work with potential authors and help them move forward with additional books. People like stories, especially rags to riches or overcoming the seemingly impossible. With Don Piper, *90 Minutes in Heaven* has, of course, been the best seller, but three other books followed that one. Once people knew who Don was, they were open to finding out what Don believed.

At the beginning of this chapter, I mentioned your talking to a fictional CEO. Even if she's not initially interested in telling her story, you can point out that her story *is* unique. You'll know her background and can demonstrate why it's a story worth telling. How did she rise to the top of the company or corporation? By telling her story, she allows readers to know who she is and how she functions. After that, if you make the CEO sympathetic and interesting (and flawed), readers are open to discover her philosophical ideas or practical solutions.

Starting with a person's story isn't always the way to go, but it's still my general rule. Immediately I think of two men for whom I wrote a total of eleven books. None of them were autobiographical. In both instances, the two men had so many excellent *and proven* ideas that their personal stories never came up as potential books.

• • •

One writer says he starts by writing to prospects and sending them three or four ideas, including a paragraph explaining each one. He doesn't always get a response, but he picks up enough business to keep him busy all year.

Because I'm more into the personal approach, I suggest you not send anything by mail or e-mail if you want it read. Make an appointment or find a way to talk to the prospective author. Connect with him at the gym or at a civic meeting. Ask a mutual friend to introduce you.

If you want to show your ideas on paper, that may work for you. When you meet, tell the prospect up front why you wanted to meet and say, "I've written down a few ideas that I think would make good books. May I show them to you?"

If the prospective client agrees, you'll include your contact information on your neatly arranged page. You might also give the person your card, but having the information on the same sheet as the ideas means that person doesn't have to search through a purse or pocket to find your card.

When I discuss book ideas with authors, I prefer to throw out ideas I have inside my head. A few times I've thrown out a concept, and the person tagged that with something he liked. That's always exciting to me.

In college, I learned the principle of thesis, antithesis, and synthesis. Adapting this to the field of ghostwriting, the triad goes like this.

You start with the thesis—that's the concept or proposition.

The CEO responds with, "That doesn't quite work for me. I was thinking more of . . ." (In classical thinking, that's the antithesis—a negation or reaction to your idea.)

"You know, I like that idea," you say, "and suppose we tweak it a little . . ." You talk further and accept the best parts of the thesis and antithesis and develop a new concept, which is called the synthesis.

I especially like that approach, because you express your ideas, and authors have the opportunity to insert theirs—thereby giving them greater ownership.

Sometimes prospective authors need only a little prodding before they open up and create their own thesis.

I've seen this occur many times at writers conferences. Even though attendees are generally not prospects, I see the triad in action. Because I'm on the faculty, I have fifteen-minute appointments with prospective scribes. The person comes to me with an idea (thesis), and I listen and say, "But what if you . . . ?" (Antithesis.)

Sometimes the writer grabs the idea I throw out and goes no further, or he may say, "I like that, and if I added . . ." (Synthesis.)

If you have ideas for an author, don't be afraid to speak out. That person may not like it (your thesis), but you will enable him to think with a new frame of reference.

I can tell you that no authors have ever laughed at my ideas. Sometimes they've said, "No, I don't think so," and I'm all right with that.

Think of it this way: the individuals you talk with are already successful on some level. (You wouldn't choose to write about someone who has failed at everything she tried, would you?) Success isn't an accident, but a mark of achievement. The person has shown resilience or ingenuity and probably is open to new ways of thinking. Use that background to offer ideas.

One businessman for whom I wrote two books said, "I get fifty ideas a week by tossing things out to my staff and listening to their responses. About one idea every three weeks is workable." He felt that was a good percentage.

TAKEAWAYS

To give ideas to an author, research the individual, and learn as much as you can before you make contact.

- Find a way to connect with the person.
- Don't assume that a personal-experience book is the place to start.
- Be prepared to throw out several ideas. (Begin the thesis triad.)
- Listen carefully to the prospect's responses.

17

YOU CAN SAY NO
TO AUTHORS

To become a successful collaborator, you have to be able to say no at times. That may not be easy. I believe in being direct with prospective clients and giving them specific reasons for declining.

I consider this chapter important, because many beginning collaborators will grab anything that comes their way. My rule from the beginning has been that if I can't get enthusiastic about the topic, I don't want to consider it. And yes, I did become excited about projects that didn't sell, but I believe I did the best job in writing them that I knew how.

I know a few collaborators who don't respond to queries that don't interest them. If prospective clients contact me, I follow the golden rule here and try to think how I would feel if someone didn't reply to my inquiry.

Below is an e-mail I sent to a prospective client in February of 2013, who contacted me after reading *90 Minutes in Heaven*. My opening paragraph pointed out several positives in the author's idea but said I was unable to take on the project. Then I wrote the following paragraphs:

> You and your family have a powerful story. Despite that, I want to point out big problems you need to consider.
>
> 1. There are many stories somewhat similar to yours. That doesn't invalidate yours, but such stories are reported all the time. [I made reference to Don Piper's book and compared it to others on the market.]
>
> 2. Personal-experience books aren't selling well. My agent recently told me that they must be extraordinary and unlike others already in print. Although you have some significant things you want told, they're not unique.
>
> 3. The publishing industry has changed in the past few years. Today when people write a book, they need to be able to go on the road to promote it by speaking and doing interviews. The continued success of *90 Minutes in Heaven* is largely because Don Piper speaks more than two hundred times a year. Publishers call this "platform" or "identity," and unless you know how to sell thousands of books, most publishers aren't interested.
>
> 4. Because publishers don't know what's going to happen with electronic books versus paper, they have cut back on the books they acquire and currently are quite cautious.

All this must sound discouraging—that's not my purpose. If you know the situation clearly, you can make a wiser decision.

Furthermore, as I stated above, I can't take on any more projects, but if you feel you want to pursue this, I can refer you to other writers, and they will probably suggest self-publishing. Although you can do that now, you would still have the burden of selling your books. Today print-on-demand (POD) publishing allows you to buy as few copies at a time as you wish— which could help.

If I refer you, those writers will expect you to pay for their services, usually half in advance. I can't tell you the amount, because it varies, but that's something you need to consider.

If you want the name of a writer, I'll be delighted to connect you. Or if you have further questions, please e-mail me again.

Some never respond to me; a few thank me for taking time to explain. I don't want to hurt anyone's feelings or discourage inquirers. I remind myself that I may be mistaken. So far I haven't turned down a project that became a best seller.

An important thing I want to point out in saying no is that writers receive money for their work, and not all prospective authors come with that understanding.

During my first years of collaborating, several people approached me to write books for them. They were sure their book would sell a million copies and we'd both be rich. They promised to pay me *after* the sale of the books.

Once, as I've previously mentioned, a man responded to my turning him down by saying, "But you're a Christian, and God gave you a gift to use for others." He made it clear that he didn't expect to pay me because I was only serving Jesus Christ in exercising my spiritual gift.

"You're right that God gifted me," I said, "but God also says that workers are worthy to receive pay for what they do." I referred to the Old Testament reference not to muzzle the ox that plowed the field and quoted Paul's words to Timothy, "Workers deserve their wages."[17]

Like other professionals, I refuse when the topic doesn't interest me. For instance, within months after the death of Michael Jackson, a man who had been close to the singer wanted me to help him write a behind-the-scenes story of the fabled singer. I wasn't interested in any kind of exposé.

Besides that, something about the man didn't ring true to me, which was my second reason for saying no. Later I read an item on the Internet that stated that a few months before he died, Michael Jackson had fired him. And it printed a copy of the letter.

Over the years I've ghosted diet books (even though I'm slender and have never been on a diet) because I'm interested in health and fitness. I'm open to learning more about topics that interest me. I once wrote a book on suicide prevention because I wanted to understand why people could feel despondent enough to take their own lives.

• • •

---

17   1 Timothy 5:18.

"I don't think you have enough material for a book," is a common statement I write in my refusal. Usually the person has had *one* powerful, dramatic experience, and I could handle that in one chapter. My question to them is, "And then what happened?"

I point out that people want to know what happened afterward. "How have you used that tragedy or great experience in your life?" Too often it remains a strong but isolated event.

At times prospects come to me because they've spoken somewhere and people have said to them, "You ought to have a book." But what they say in their thirty-minute presentation may be the whole story. Although exciting and informative, there may be nothing more.

Years ago I heard an evangelist tell how God had healed him so that he could see out of his right eye even though it was an empty socket. He related a powerful story of how he had lost the eye through cancer and how deeply he and others had prayed for his healing. Then the miracle occurred.

He had one sermon—a testimony of God touching him. That was it. Hardly enough for what I'd call a book, even though he preached in many churches. He also admitted that he never went back to a congregation, because he didn't have anything else.

You also need to be firm in turning a person down. In my first days of collaborating, that was difficult for me because I hate rejections. But I decided that I owed people the truth—tempered with kindness.

● ● ●

Publishers want books by authors who are promotable, that is, who have a platform. Authors need to be able to speak in public, do interviews, and have huge followings on social media. The authors have to be their own promoters, and not many people can do that.

If your prospect has good material and is promotable but has no platform, make suggestions to help him build that platform. It's a little extra work to tell him, but it's also an act of kindness.

I also remind myself that by taking on work I didn't want, I'm not open for projects that I do want.

TAKEAWAYS

- If you aren't enthusiastic about the topic, say no.
- If you decide to say no to her, respond and offer an explanation.
- If you think the work is viable but not for you, refer him to another writer.
- Make sure the prospect understands that writers charge for their service.
- If you don't think there's enough material for a book, be honest in saying so.
- Bear in mind that publishers not only want material they can sell, but they want authors who have a platform.
- Be firm but kind in turning down unwanted projects.

18

YOU WILL EXPERIENCE REJECTIONS

In the beginning of your career, you may be tempted to grab at anything, eager to have contracts and build a resume.

Be cautious. I took on a few attempts for books that didn't work out because the clients wanted me to write a proposal for a royalty publisher. I was flattered and excited to be asked.

We were turned down by every publisher we queried. The authors refused to go to vanity publishing (as we called self-publishing or independent publishing in the 1980s), and that was the end.

Two results came from those three or four bad experiences.

First, when a book didn't sell to a royalty publisher, I struggled with guilt because I felt as if I had failed. I had received payment for writing the proposal, and I had been sure a publisher would buy the manuscript. Otherwise I wouldn't have accepted the offer. That made me feel a sense of personal failure. In retrospect, each time the editors were correct in refusing to buy.

Second, for the first decade of collaborating, I didn't have enough discernment (or call it experience) to grasp what made editors buy or reject my proposals. Several times the news came back, "We've just contracted for a book on that topic." A few times publishers responded, "We like the book, and we'd like to publish it. But we put out a book with the same general material five years ago, and it bombed." Sometimes the publishers simply said, "We've decided to pass."

Right here I should probably tell you, "Try not to take the rejection personally." That's nonsense. Of course you will—at first. Perhaps for a long time. But if you persist and continue to mature, rejections will lose their power to crush you. In fact, you'll assume that not every publisher will want your work.

No matter what the response, it took me years to get beyond a sense of failure—and I'm probably a slow learner on that matter. But eventually I was able to say, "I'm trying to sell them a *product*, and it's not something they want. The rejection isn't a personal attack on me but their lack of interest in the project."

A memorable moment for me was around 2005, when I taught at the Ridgecrest Writers Conference, which was the last year Yvonne Lehmann led the conference.

One evening she talked about rejections and asked everyone to stand. She started out by saying, "If you've never submitted or never had a rejection, sit down." Then she said, "If you have had just one rejection, sit down." She went to "five or less." By the time she finished, only three people were standing: Sandy Brooks, Davis Bunn, and me.

Sandy said she had received a thousand rejections, which topped Davis and me. Even so, I think it was important for conferees to see that the most successful writers at the conference were those with the most rejections.

In the days when I was still struggling over rejections, someone sent me a wonderful quotation by novelist Barbara Kingsolver. I liked it so much that I printed it, laminated it, and kept it taped on the right corner of my desk for at least a year.

> This manuscript of yours that has just come back from another editor is a precious package. Don't consider it rejected. Consider that you've addressed it "to the editor who can appreciate my work," and it has simply come back stamped "Not at this address." Just keep looking for the right address.

• • •

In my early days of writing, I started an editing group called the Scribe Tribe. Even though I wasn't always able to follow my own suggestions we lovingly-but-brutally tore each other's work apart. Here's one lesson I taught and struggled to accept myself: if a refusal had anything encouraging written on it, we'd call it a nonacceptance letter instead of a rejection. (In those days we did everything with typewriters and through the US postal service.)

For instance, an editor might write at the bottom of a form rejection, "Try us again," or, "We almost bought this. Maybe next time we will."

A few years later—once I learned to handle rejections—I wrote ten suggestions for the Scriptiques, a second editing group I founded.

1. Be patient but persist. Those who succeed in the writing business are those who keep at it for years, despite rejection and setback, and who think and plan in terms of decades.

2. All writers have their work rejected sometimes; most have it rejected frequently. Whether you like it or not, rejection is an inevitable part of being a professional writer.

3. Try not to take rejection personally. Your *manuscript* is being rejected, not you. A rejection reflects only on the work you've submitted, not on your overall ability or promise as a writer.

4. You can get a manuscript rejected for countless reasons. Many of them have nothing to do with the quality of the work itself. Publications change focus or policies. Editors move. Pieces scheduled for publications get pulled when an extra full-page ad comes in.

5. Don't allow rejection to shake your faith in a piece or in yourself. If you believe in something you've written, keep sending it out—dozens of times if necessary—until it's accepted. Sometimes manuscripts get accepted after twenty or more rejections.

6. Don't accept editors' words as infallible. They're not always good critics. Their comments (if they write anything) are sometimes hastily written and without much thought.

7. If the editor rejects your piece but offers comments meant to help you rewrite or write a new one, read those words carefully.

8. If the editor rejects your manuscript but says positive or encouraging things, send that editor something else. If the editor says the piece came close, consider rewriting it and sending it back.

9. Never tell an editor that you've had a piece rejected before.

10. Don't call or write editors to argue the merits of a rejected piece. Instead, use your energy to send the manuscript to other publishers.

All ten of these items came out of my own experience except the last one: I've never argued about a rejection. For me, when an editor says no, I consider that a death notice.

• • •

When people approach me, especially in person, one of my gifts *and failings* is that I easily relate to them, even if their ideas are awful. In the early years I caught their enthusiasm and was hooked into their thinking. Their excitement transferred over to me, and I was ready to change the world by writing their books.

Eventually I realized that I couldn't trust my emotions to make a wise decision right then. I had to pull back and look at the situation objectively.

Two things helped. My late wife was an overworked editor of curriculum with a publishing house, but when I occasionally mentioned a book project, she listened. Shirley was a quiet woman and sometimes simply said, "I don't think you'll be able to sell that." I can't think of a time when she was wrong.

The second was my agent, Deidre Knight. She has always been kind enough to listen when I've come up with a writing project. She's a superb agent with keen instincts, and if she says, "Don't do it," or, "I don't know if I can sell it," I listen.

Deidre hasn't always been right, and she's not infallible. Once we were both excited over a project, sure it would sell, but it didn't, even though both of us believed in it. That happens.

I read somewhere that top agents sell about 75 percent of their projects. That means they're not always successful. They also struggle with rejection. I mention that because now and then a disgruntled writer says, "My agent couldn't get me a contract."

Don't blame the agent. She probably has enough internal guilt without your adding to it.

TAKEAWAYS

- Be patient but persist.
- Most writers have their work rejected sometimes; most have it rejected frequently.
- Try not to take rejection personally.
- You can get a manuscript rejected for countless reasons.
- Don't allow rejection to shake your faith in a piece or in yourself.
- Don't accept editors' words as infallible.
- If the editor rejects your work but offers comments meant to help you rewrite or write a new piece, read those words carefully.
- If the editor rejects a manuscript but says positive or encouraging things, send that editor something else.
- Never tell an editor that you've had a piece rejected before.
- Don't call or write editors to argue the merits of a rejected piece.

19

WHAT'S YOUR TITLE?

When nonwriters ask me to help with their book, they nearly always have "a dynamite title." I put that in quotes because no matter what it is, they're sure it's perfect. *The Lord Is My Husband* came from one of my writer friends in our early days. The publisher wisely called the book *Divorced!*

One title that an author came to me with was *It's Easier to Succeed than to Fail.* The book certainly didn't reflect that, and I couldn't convince him of the odd logic. He also headed a large private corporation and bought thousands of copies, so that became the title. I still didn't like it.

These quirky titles come about because the authors thought of them, liked them, and were positive everyone would love them.

To offset that, at my first meeting with clients, I usually say to the person who has the perfect title, "Don't become inflexible with your title. Let's leave it for now, and after we've worked on the book, we'll look objectively and think about whether that's still the best one." Except for with the title mentioned above, the authors have listened.

Think of the people some call gatekeepers between your writing someone's book and consumers reading it. The material goes from you to the author, to your agent, to your editor, to your publisher's editorial board, to your publisher's sales reps, to bookstore chains, to warehouse clubs, and to discounters like Target or Sam's Club. If any of them don't like the title, regardless of previous responses to it, your suggestions or input won't matter.

Some publishers spend as much time focusing on a book's title as they do a marketing plan.

I've read in several places that the average reader spends about two seconds looking at a title on a book table. (I suspect it's less than that.) Regardless, it means that unless someone already knows about your title or the author, you have only a brief moment in which to grab that consumer.

• • •

So now I'll tell you how I work with titles. My proposals go to my agent. She may not like the title, and if she doesn't, I listen carefully. Several times she's come up with a far better title than I had. In those cases, I probably developed the same problem as the authors: I'm too close to the subject to be objective.

Once my agent and I agree on the title, she sends the proposal to her hit list of editors—those she thinks would like the book.

On my third book with Don Piper, our title was *The New Normal.* Ten years ago that was a new concept and was the scope of the book—living a new life when the old one is destroyed. Our editor insisted we had to use the word *heaven* in the title to connect it with *90 Minutes in Heaven.* They called it *Heaven Is Real.*

That title doesn't fit the book. It sold well at first and hit the *New York Times* best-seller list—for one week. Several years later a similar title came out called *Heaven Is for Real*. I'm not sure, but I suspect we sold a number of copies of our book because people thought they had the story of Todd Burpo.

Sometimes you just can't come up with the right title. Don't fight it. Let the title emerge as you work on the manuscript.

When I work on a book, the publisher may occasionally give me a title. For example, the publisher decided on *Bloodline: The John Turnipseed Story* before I wrote it. Otherwise, I ignore the title the author suggests, work on the book, and let it emerge. When I'm unsure of a title, I have two ways of letting my unconscious mind work—or, as I like to think, waiting for God to whisper to me.

First, I've been an avid runner for nearly forty years. My running in the dark, usually around four thirty in the morning, is what I call sacred time—time just for God and me. If I need a title, I think about it early in the run and then let it go. Near the end of my run, the title often pops into my head. If it doesn't that day, it will on another morning. I let my subconscious mind work while I run. That's how I came up with the title *90 Minutes in Heaven*.

Second, I hear the whisper in the twilight zone. In those moments the title comes to me. Maybe that's only my subconscious at work; I like to think of it as God answering me.

Sometimes, afraid that I'll forget it, I rush to my computer and type it.

Even if editors change the titles, I still come up with my own.

Here's my secret about titles: *I write a title for the editor, not for the consumer.* I want an editor to get an idea of what the book is about, even if that title doesn't appear on the published copy.

For instance, the first book I did with Salome Thomas-EL I called *I Choose to Stay: A Black Teacher Refuses to Desert the Inner City.* I thought it was a fairly good title, but I was sure that after Kensington bought it, they would change it. They didn't. And the book sold well.

My best-known books are *Gifted Hands: The Ben Carson Story* and *90 Minutes in Heaven: A True Story of Death and Life.* The editor reversed my subtitle from *A True Story of Life and Death*—which was stronger, even though I'm not sure many readers noticed that *death* came before *life.*

The other title, *Gifted Hands,* was difficult for me and even tougher for the original publisher. I wanted the title to reflect the work of Ben Carson, a pediatric neurosurgeon who had an amazing ability to see things three-dimensionally. His gift is a marvelous eye-and-hand coordination, although he said modestly, "Any good surgeon can do that."

How do you put eye-and-hand coordination in a title? *Gifted Hands* was the best I could come up with. The editors didn't like it and sent me a list of twenty-seven suggestions. I disliked every one. I said that, but told them I'd agree to whatever they chose.

They came back to my original title. I didn't consider that a great victory, except that it told me my title worked, which boosted my self-confidence. About that time I read an interview with Jerry Jenkins in which he said that some people have a knack for good titles and others don't.

I think Jerry was correct, and I've struggled to come up with good titles. After selling nearly 140 books, I think I have a feel for them. It also gives me great respect for the difficulty in making such decisions.

• • •

The first suggestion for choosing titles I ever received was from the late Bruce Larson. "If the title says or implies *you*, it's a good title." And his books sold. Two of his I especially liked were *Dare to Live Now* and *Dance with Me*.

Here are my principles for writing titles for nonfiction books.

1. Grab attention and make a promise. That's what the top advertisers do. *Ten Ways to Save Your Marriage* or the once-famous *Thirty Days to a More Powerful Vocabulary* are good examples.

Although I don't list it as a principle, some words are weighty in titles, and *powerful* is one of them. Try to sneak in a strong verb or adjective.

2. Solve a problem. Immediately I think of books that sold well using that concept: *You Are Not Alone*, *Have a New Kid by Friday*, and *Living After Divorce*. Those titles say or imply that you have the answer to a felt need or problem.

3. Write a clear, unambiguous title. Years ago someone told me about a book called *Secret Lovers*. Like most people, I emphasized the first word, *secret*, and assumed the book was a romance. However, the title was misleading because it referred to those who loved secrets. No wonder the book failed—it was about decoding during World War II.

If your title isn't clear, potential buyers may not find your book, because it will be improperly shelved, or they may not realize it's a subject of interest to them. Make a title easy to read, like *Courage Under Fire* or *A Tale of Two Cities*.

4. Make your title specific, short, and easy to remember. A classic film is called *Rebel Without a Cause*. When I ghosted Franklin Graham's autobiography, the publisher chose the title *Rebel with a Cause*. Memorable? For people who knew the film it may have worked—or it may have confused them. Sometimes, even nearly twenty years later, people will say to me, "I read *Rebel without a Cause* that you wrote for Franklin Graham."

I smile, glad they made some kind of connection.

Literary agent Jeff Herman once said, "No more than five words." His point was people buy books by impulse. A long title makes readers stop and think.

5. Think in pictures. Good titles are visual, such as *The Last Man on Earth*, *12 Years a Slave*, *Woman on Death Row*, and *Sleep Your Way to Weight Loss*.

6. Make the title words pronounceable. I wrote a book called *Prayer Fitness*—okay, not a great title—but it came out in the early 1980s when physical fitness became a big issue. The publisher changed the title, but it was unpronounceable for many: *Prayerobics*. That probably wouldn't be as much of a problem today. Back then people asked, "How do you pronounce it?"

The story goes that Robert Ludlum wrote a novel titled *The Wolfsschanze Covenant*, but his editors wisely changed it to something readers could say and called it *The Holcroft Covenant*.

7. Make sure your title fits the type, theme, and mood of the book. I once talked with a woman who showed me her

newly self-published book *If God Loves Me, Why Can't I Find a Husband?* A rather cutesy title, but it didn't fit the book. I skimmed the first two chapters and realized it was a heavy-handed theological treatise on God's love for us. It didn't occur to her that she was misleading anyone who looked at her 337 pages.

"I thought it would grab attention," she said in defense.

"It does, but in advertising I'd call it bait and switch," I said. "Your title is a promise not only of content, but it indicates the style or mood of your book."

"I still think it's a good title," she said, snatched the book from my hand, and walked away.

8. In nonfiction, use the title to grab attention, and let the subtitle explain. That was the purpose of the subtitle *A True Story of Death and Life* for *90 Minutes in Heaven*.

• • •

Here are a few additional thoughts to bear in mind when writing titles:

- Think of titles as headlines.
- Too often readers, editors, and agents read only titles before selecting what to read next.
- Focus on key phrases or lists such as *Live 10 Healthy Years Longer* or *Five Love Languages*.
- Some titles are double entendres—a figure of speech or particular way of wording to be understood in either of two ways or to have a *double* meaning, such as Alan Watts's *In My Own Way*. Years ago there was a TV series called *Family Matters*. I didn't watch the show, but I liked the double entendre.

- A once-familiar method was to use oblique biblical references such as *Our Vines Have Tender Grapes*, *The Sun Also Rises*, *East of Eden*, and *The Grapes of Wrath*. Because we live in a biblically illiterate culture, be careful about using such references today.
- Avoid vague, general titles such as *A Sudden Meaning* or *A Long Trip*.

• • •

No one can copyright titles, and sometimes you'll see five or six books with the same title.

Years ago a Charles Bronson flick called *Telefon* (and spelled that way) referred several times to the Robert Frost poem from the 1920s "The Road Not Taken." One of the lines refers to "promises to keep." Whether it was a direct result of that film or the book by Walter Wager, I don't know, but I looked in what was called *Books in Print* and found seven books, all in print, carrying the title *Promises to Keep*. And, so far as I could tell, all of them were romances.

If you think you have a good title, go to Amazon.com or Barnesandnoble.com. Type in your title, and you'll see if someone else has used it. Also search for a site that uses the same words.

TAKEAWAYS

- You can't copyright titles.
- Urge authors not to be inflexible with their proposed titles.
- If you don't have a good title, work on the book, and let it emerge.

When selecting a title, here are ideas for you to consider.
- Use or imply *you* in the title.
- Grab attention and make a promise.
- Solve a problem.
- Write a clear, unambiguous title.
- Make your title specific, short, and easy to remember.
- Think in pictures. Good titles are visual.
- Make the title words pronounceable.
- Make sure your title fits the type, theme, and mood of the book.
- In nonfiction, use the title to grab attention, and let the subtitle explain.

20

WATCH YOUR VOCABULARY

You probably have a more extensive vocabulary than the author for whom you write. (You are the wordsmith, and words are your tools.) That's both a plus and a minus.

As a sensitive writer, you probably have a preference for using either *start* or *begin*. You might have a number of synonyms you like to use such as *launch* or *commence*. For you, there are slight nuances that you feel even if you can't explain why.

That's the plus for your writing. Your familiarity with the tools of your craft helps you make such distinctions. And it doesn't stop after ten years if you're a growing writer. For instance, after more than twenty-five years, I realized I often wrote *when* and I meant *after*.

Take this sentence: "When Mason returned home, he ate dinner." Perfectly understandable but not technically correct. To my thinking, *when* implies *at that time*, meaning that at the moment Mason returned home, he ate dinner. At the same time? It probably happened later. Even though I still use that construction frequently, my sensitivity to the difference makes me cringe if someone uses *when* in that way.

You probably have your own self-discoveries that make you a better writer. That's what we expect of professionals. You're always learning and improving.

• • •

The downside of an extensive vocabulary is that you may tend to use some of those words most people don't know. Although quite normal for you, they may be alien to your client. Your role is to work with the author. Use your client's special phrases in place of your own.

In chapter 10, I wrote about one of my worst experiences of being a ghostwriter. The author and his personal assistant sat across the room from me while he read every sentence aloud. Occasionally he completed a full paragraph before he paused and commented.

Although it took me nearly a year to get the book done because of that style, I learned something valuable. When he stumbled on a word, I immediately underlined it on my laptop. A few times he said, "I don't even know what that word means."

He caught me.

I was too naïve or not experienced enough to argue. The first time it happened, I had used the word *rationale*. I tried to explain its meaning by using a number of words, among them *foundation*, *basis*, *reasoning*, and *motivation*. Then I asked him, "How would you say it?"

"How about *logic*?"

As a wordsmith, that synonym wasn't quite what I wanted him to say, but it was his choice, and the word felt right to him.

"It's your book, and I want it to express you," I said and added, "*Logic* it is," while making the change on my laptop.

• • •

Another factor is being sensitive to the pet words the author uses. All of us have words we say. When I was a student at the School for Military Justice during my days in the US Navy, we were in formation on the parade ground every morning at eight o'clock. Our commanding officer spoke for about three minutes. I think it was his version of a pep-up-the-troops talk. He was brilliant, and I liked him. After a few mornings, however, I realized he had four or five most-favored words.

The one that struck me most (which I didn't know at the time) was *cognizant*. Although I picked up the meaning from context, it was a wonderful word that I looked up in a dictionary and tucked away inside my mental vocabulary file. (In case you're as ignorant as I was, it means to be aware or to have knowledge about something.)

After I caught on, I played a game in my head every morning and counted the number of times "Commander Cognizant" used his pet word. It was rarely less than three times.

That illustrates the point I want to make of your being *cognizant* of overworked words and terms. In 1989, I worked with one of the most fascinating men I've ever met, Norman Vaughn, on his book *With Byrd at the Bottom of the World*. Published in 1990, it's still in print. A bright, articulate man with an amazing depth of knowledge, he was also one of the most upbeat people I've ever known.

And Norm had one special word. *Great.* And usually spoken so that it required an exclamation mark after it. To my chagrin, I became so caught up in listening and trying to retain his voice that I missed that repetitive occurrence.

From the beginning of my writing days, I've never sent out a manuscript without someone looking it over and proofreading it. I hired Harriett, the woman who edited my first book, to edit the Vaughn book.

Nearly two weeks later, I went to pick up the manuscript, and Harriett asked, "Do you realize how many times you use *great* in this book?"

"No, I hadn't noticed."

She showed me one page of hard copy where she had circled the word seven times. On one page! I was embarrassed but grateful. When I went back to my computer to check, I did a word search and discovered that I had used it 207 times.

For most of us, the rule of word usage is not to employ the same word twice in a paragraph. Some would say not more than three times on a page. Obviously, there are exceptions, but it's a good principle. And one of the things I'm still learning is that even when I go over my final draft before sending it for proofing, my longtime proofreader, Wanda Rosenberry, catches the repetition three or four times in my manuscript. But I'm improving.

TAKEAWAYS

- You probably have a larger vocabulary than your authors. Stay with their word preferences.
- Look for the expressions you favor, and notice how often you use them.
- Remind yourself that the author's word choice comes first.
- Learn your client's favorite words, but don't overuse them.

21

YOU WILL DO RESEARCH

For a ghosted book, whether an autobiography, a book on diet-ing, or a manual on how to have a maintenance-free yard, the project involves research. Normally the author has the experi-ence and knowledge and provides *most* of the material for you. Most.

This allows you to accumulate needed facts much faster than if you had to do everything yourself. A major reason I do this kind of writing is because the experts can provide the material I need. If I researched everything for books I ghosted, it would definitely slow down the process.

Because you want an outstanding manuscript, you'll also do additional reading or research on the topic. Think of readers who know less about the subject or the person than you do. What questions would they ask? What information would they want? Make it a rule to know far more than you put into the manuscript.

• • •

CECIL MURPHEY

Most collaborators have at least one strange experience, and I want to share mine. In 2003, a highly successful entrepreneur in San Jose, California, contacted me. He said he'd read three of my books, liked the way I wrote, and wanted to hire me. "I have twenty-nine books I want to publish," he told me, "and I want you to write them."

Without my having to ask, he said he'd fly me to San Jose so we could meet and get acquainted. I liked the man. He offered me quite a large amount of money for each of the books. When he told me the subject of several he wanted written, I said, "Those aren't topics I know much about, but I'm willing to learn."

I tried to explain how I operated, such as that I taped the material. He said he was sure that however I worked, it would be satisfactory, and he dismissed the subject.

Because I was finishing a project, it was almost a month before I was free to return. After I came into his office, I set up my recording equipment, and he told me, in about five sentences, what he wanted me to write.

He stood up and started to leave the room.

"Wait a minute—aren't you going to give me the material?"

He stared at me. "I tell you the topic, and you write the book."

That was a terribly awkward moment, and I said, "That's not how I work. I assumed you understood my process." Then I explained that he provided the raw data, and I wrote the book.

Need I mention that I never wrote the books for him? I didn't write the first one because he was no expert on that topic—but it was a subject that interested him enough to find out. He thought it was a good topic and readers would buy.

The man from San Jose was the exception. Generally people tell me their stories or give me the information I need. For example, I did a series of books for an expert on drug addiction. He either had the information inside his head or mailed me books about it. I asked questions, and the information poured out. I compressed into four intense days what would have taken me months to learn on my own.

Until then I had known little about drug addiction, and he had the educational background and practical experience to talk about what happened to brain chemicals when people used drugs. Fascinating material and a wonderful learning experience for me. In fact, some of the things he told me I'm sure I'd never have been able to find because he quoted scholarly journals and then broke down what they meant into language I could understand.

I was able to write his book in less than three months because I depended on his material and didn't have to buy books or spend time on research to correct my abysmal ignorance.

Not only was it fascinating and financially profitable, it was a marvelous learning experience.

• • •

This is a good place to mention one major reason I'm able to make a good living as a ghostwriter. The authors provide most of the information I'll need, so I save hours—days—of reading and processing.

Because of turnaround speed, collaboration makes it advantageous for authors like me to make a good full-time living. Another factor, of course, is that I do everything quickly.

When I lived in Kenya, the Africans called me *Haraka*, which means fast or speedy.

Not every writer thinks and types rapidly, so be kind to yourself if you're slow at the task. It doesn't make either of us superior, only different.

The book I mentioned above that I completed in three months would have taken me at least seven or eight on my own and possibly a year. And because I wasn't an expert in drug addiction, I'm certain I would have left out significant details.

TAKEAWAYS

- All projects involve some research.
- The authors, who are experts, provide most of the information for you.
- You want to do an outstanding job, so you'll also do additional reading or research on the topic.
- Depending on your writing speed, it's possible to make a good living by being a collaborator.

22

YES, YOU WILL HAVE A CONTRACT

All ghostwriters have contracts. Always. Without exception.

That means: get it in writing. Insist on a written agreement as the number-one rule of any arrangement you make with authors. *You will have a contract.* You don't have to go to a lawyer, but have your terms clearly stated as well as who will be responsible for each item. And I mention them below.

I don't include confidentiality in my contracts, because I feel that's a different issue. If any author were to ask, I wouldn't hesitate to add it. Even from my first books, I've assured the authors that I wouldn't reveal anything private without their permission.

You and any prospective authors need to discuss issues that might arise in the course of your collaboration. Talk to any victim of a failed collaboration, however, and you'll hear the same cry: "If only we had had a contract."

Some writers consider it an insult to ask someone they already know to sign a formal contract. I tell them, "Think of the contract as a way of laying out *clearly* what you and the author can expect from each other. A contract acknowledges that what you are about to undertake is not only a mutually enjoyable project, but a business arrangement."

Developing a contract before you start working together is the best possible way to protect both of you from future misunderstandings. Circumstances, interests, and enthusiasms may change for either of you; a contract can prevent that adjustment from turning into a major conflict.

By spelling out the terms of your collaboration in some form, each becomes answerable to the agreement rather than to the other person. For me, the best part has been that I haven't had to nag for compliance. On only a couple of occasions have I pointed back to the contract, and that settled the issues.

Ghostwriting projects begin with the best intentions. Someone has an idea or area of expertise that, paired with your writing skills, should lead to success. However, projects don't always end with that same upbeat feeling.

You don't need to incorporate legal language. I call my contracts a covenant agreement, and I haven't had any problems. It is not as much a legal matter as it is stating what you expect of the authors and what they can anticipate from you, the writer.

You list everything you will do (such as when you'll deliver a first draft of the book).

You also explain the payment plan. Most writers ask for half up front and the rest when the project is finished and the author is satisfied with your work. (Some ask for a third to start, a third with the delivery of a full rough draft, and the final third at the end.)

Never write a book on speculation—that is, writing the manuscript and hoping it will sell but receiving no money unless it does. This is a business; treat it that way, and don't extend credit.

Make it clear whether your name will be on the book. If it's a royalty project, who will market the book? Will you sell the book through an agent? Generally the authors don't know the business, and that task falls on the writers.

Today we sell most of our books by proposals, and I ask authors to pay me to write them. By the time I've finished the proposal, I figure I've written about 40 percent of the book. I've earned my pay.

My agent isn't involved in this stage. Usually I inform her of what I'm doing, but she waits for me to send her the completed proposal.

In my covenants I like to include an escape clause. If the person isn't happy with me or I'm not happy with the author, we need an easy way to break it off. I usually say that if either party wishes to terminate the contract, a simple letter to that effect is all it takes.

If you receive half of the agreed-on price and do your job but the author isn't satisfied, let her stop the proceedings, and don't return the money. However, if you've been paid half and later decide you don't want to do the job or can't continue, certainly return the money. You haven't earned it, and you broke the contract.

Here's my one experience in which a contract saved me from repayment. I had agreed to write a self-published book for a survivor of World War II in Eastern Europe. I did it on a three-part payment plan. After I completed the initial agreement to send him sample chapters and a synopsis, he became ill. I didn't know it was serious and wondered why he hadn't responded.

Four months later his lawyer terminated the agreement and asked me to return the initial payment. I sent him a copy of our covenant agreement, and I never heard from him again.

• • •

Money *is* a big issue. As much as you may love what you're doing, you still want to get paid for your work.

My first rule for prospective clients is to make it clear that I do not work for free. I am a professional and expect payment for my services. If you state that plainly, people will respect you more, and you will respect yourself.

Occasionally I do pro bono work, but it's my choice, and I do it when I truly believe God wants me to offer myself.

I mentioned writing the proposal and my agent sending it out. If the book sells, I start a new contract with how the author and I split the publisher's advance. Notice the word *contract*.

• • •

One of my collaborator friends wrote, "The most challenging aspect to my writing career is getting authors to appreciate the value of my work and the rates I charge for writing a book." He went on to say that it's a personal, subjective issue for the aspiring author and must be handled carefully.

"The problem in measuring the value of the work is amplified by the vast differences in prices among ghostwriters." He pointed out that he had recently checked prices on the Internet for books with sixty thousand words or roughly 250 pages. He said the prices ranged from $1,000 to $250,000.

"I mentally scratch my head," he wrote, "wondering how one writer can offer services for about $5,000, and another says $85,000 for the same project." He did admit that experience and sales record figured in. "But still the range is so big, I don't get it."

After a few more sentences, he made this interesting observation: "The high-priced rates don't concern me." He felt that beginners (and hoped that's who the cheap ones were) underpriced themselves to gain a few projects. "They don't realize it, but their low fees undercut professionals who want to make a living at the craft."

Many of those less expensive writers had spouses who financially supported them so they could work for $2,000 a year.

And I understood. At the end of his e-mail, he told me that a client had chosen one writer over him because of a difference of $2,000. "And the man he chose has never written anything for the royalty-paying market."

That's sad, of course, but it's also the way this business goes. My advice is to decide what you feel is right to charge given your experience and writing credentials. Stick to your figure.

When I was charging $25,000 for a flat-fee project, a man took me to lunch and flattered me by telling me how much he admired my writing. He had a copy of one of my books with him and asked me to sign it.

When he asked my fee, I told him.

"That's a little higher than others to whom I've spoken."

"If you like someone else, go to that person," I said. "In fact,

I can give you the contact information for two or three writers I highly recommend, and they charge less than I do."

He shook his head and said, "You don't negotiate, do you?"

"I don't because I'm terrible at doing that," I said. "The only way I can handle this is to set my price and hold to it. I know that I'll do the best I can for the price I state. If I agreed to a lower price, I'd resent being forced to take less. I'm afraid it might influence the quality of my writing."

Again he tried to negotiate, and I said, "You obviously don't appreciate the work I do—and that's all right. I promise to give you my very best."

Although he finally came around to my price, I decided not to write his book. I had been excited about working with him—until the money issue arose.

After the price came up, I sensed he wouldn't be happy paying what I wanted. Before we left I gave him names of two other writers.

• • •

If your proposal becomes a book that the author will self-publish, your contracts have already set down your terms. Before you talk fees for writing the entire book, however, you need to ask yourself a few questions:

- How long will this project take?
- How much can the author afford?
- Approximately how long a manuscript will I need to write?
- Who will be responsible for marketing the book? (If it's you, I suggest you build in additional compensation for yourself.)

The Informal Covenant

After I meet the client in person and agree to write the book, I follow up with my informal covenant in letter form. This is one I wrote in 2005:

When we met for dinner Wednesday evening, I outlined the basis for our working together to prepare a book proposal to send to my agent. I want to repeat those items in this letter so that it becomes our covenantal agreement.

1. I will write a book proposal for you, using the general format my agent requires. This includes two sample chapters, an overview of the book, information about you, explanation of the intended market, and an annotated bibliography of competitive books. I will submit my writing to you in rough-draft form for your changes and approval before it goes into a final form for submission.

2. After you have approved the entire proposal, I will submit it to my literary agent, Deidre Knight of The Knight Agency.

3. From the time I have received adequate material from you for the book until the presentation of the final proposal, I anticipate a period of approximately two months.

4. For the work of this proposal, my fee is $xxxx. If you agree to the terms I've laid out in this letter, your check for $ [one-half] will serve as a covenantal agreement. The remaining $ [half] will be payable when you are satisfied with the final proposal. Please make check payable to: xxxx

> 5. We have agreed that if my literary agent sells this book, she will take 15 percent commission first. You and I will then split the rest of the royalty equally. [Note: on foreign rights, if she uses a sub-agent, the commission runs 20–25 percent.]
>
> 6. Assuming my agent sells the manuscript, the authorship of the book will read: by xxxx with Cecil Murphey.
>
> 7. If at any point you wish to withdraw from this agreement, a letter or verbal statement is sufficient.

If you want help with the legal aspects, I suggest you contact Lloyd Jassin, an entertainment lawyer in New York. My agent put me in contact with him because an author tried to take advantage of me and cut out my royalties.

Mr. Jassin handled the matter quickly and effectively with one letter. Check out his website at www.CopyLaw.com.

Anne Wayman offers helpful advice on contracts. Her name came from two of my contacts. You can find her at www.about-freelancewriting.com/2009/05/ghostwriting-elements-of-my-contracts-or-letters-of-agreement. If you go to Ivan Holman's site, www.ivanhoffman.com/helpful, under the title of "Articles for Writers and Publishers," you'll find examples of contracts.

TAKEAWAYS

- Never forget: all ghostwriters have contracts. Get it in writing.
- Even if you work with a friend, you need a contract. This is business.
- Your contract spells out the responsibilities of both partners, including duties and money.
- Never write a book on speculation—payment when the book sells.
- Make it clear whether your name will appear on the cover and title page.
- Provide for an escape clause in your contracts in case either you or the author is unhappy.
- You do not return any money paid to you.
- Set your prices. Don't negotiate. If you take a lesser amount, you may be dissatisfied, and it can affect your work.

Before you talk fees, answer for yourself:
- How long will this project take?
- How much can the author afford?
- Approximately how long a manuscript will I need to write?
- Who will be responsible for marketing the book?

23

CAN YOU BE SUED?

Yes, you can be sued.

A ghostwriter friend of mine in Atlanta went to a small claims court in July of 2014, over a disgruntled client. She had ghosted his book but couldn't sell it. He sued her, insisting he went into debt to pay her because she assured him she could get a publisher for him. She had a contract, and there was nothing in it that promised she could sell the book. She won the case.

But what if she hadn't had a contract?

Twenty years ago a literary lawyer spoke to a group of us writers and said, "Never underestimate the greed of your friends." He explained that we live in a litigious society. To sue and win is easy money—or at least it looks that way.

So here you are writing a book, and the author insists on naming names and making harsh judgments in it about some of the people with whom she worked. You assume she could be sued, but what about you, the writer? Or the publisher, for putting out such a book?

Most publishers today require a signoff for anyone named in the book, even if the author says nothing negative. I have a form that I modify to fit each book.

Below are examples of signoff forms I've used. If you have permission from named individuals in the book, you're protected.

Example 1

XXXX will publish my book, *XXXX,* in early 2012.

I wish to quote you in chapter 3. I've attached the chapter and highlighted your name.

If you're agreeable, please sign and date the request below, and return a copy to me.

I hereby grant permission to Cecil Murphey to quote me as outlined above.

Signature _____

Date   _____

Example 2

When our publisher wanted to put out a special edition of *90 Minutes in Heaven* by including new stories, I sent out the following to people who had sent e-mails to Don Piper. This went out under Don's name (and every person agreed to the request). This is slightly more formal than the others because the publisher's lawyers modified it.

February 9, 2010

Dear _____:

I am the author of *90 Minutes in Heaven*. My publisher, Baker Publishing Group, wants to put out a special edition of the book and include a section called "Letters from the Gulf."

This is to request you to grant permission to me, Baker Publishing Group, and their licensees, successors and assigns, to include the material indicated below in all editions and derivations of the work in all languages throughout the world and in the advertising and promotion thereof in all media now known or hereafter devised.

Credit will be given in the form you specify below, either on the same page with the photos, on the copyright page, or in a separate section for credits.

In signing below, you represent that you are the sole owner of the rights granted herein and that the material indicated below does not infringe upon the copyright, privacy right, or other rights of anyone.

Please sign a copy of this and send it to my coauthor, Cecil Murphey. [And I list my e-mail and phone number.]

Please print your name:

_____

Please sign your name:

_____

CECIL MURPHEY

Example 3

When I wrote *Stolen: The True Story of a Sex Trafficking Survivor* for Katariina Rosenblatt, this is the form we sent to anybody we mentioned by name in the book, and it was sent as if coming from Katariina:

> You were an important part of my healing journey, and I would like to give you credit.
>
> In my book *Stolen: The True Story of a Sex Trafficking Survivor*, I use your name. I've attached the unedited version of my manuscript where I did so. If you will sign the permission slip below and fax it back to me or indicate your approval by e-mail, I would appreciate it.
>
> I give my permission to Katariina Rosenblatt and Cecil Murphey to use my name in their book, *Stolen: The True Story of a Sex Trafficking Survivor*. I understand that I am giving permission for worldwide, unlimited, nonexclusive rights in all printings/editions and adaptations.
>
> Name (print)
>
> _____
>
> Signed
>
> _____

In this letter, I mentioned *unedited version* because we knew it might change slightly. No one objected.

Example 4

The following letter went to eleven people who contributed stories to the tenth-anniversary edition of *90 Minutes in Heaven*.

July 9, 2013

Dear_____,

My name is Cecil Murphey, and I helped Don Piper write *90 Minutes in Heaven*. Baker Publishing Group plans to publish a special ten-year anniversary edition of *90 Minutes in Heaven* in early 2014.

You sent Don an e-mail after having read the book. We will include a few unique testimonies for the new edition. Your story is one we want to consider.

On the attachment, you'll see your testimony. You didn't write it for publication, so I've edited it to fit our requirements. If you'll allow us to consider using it—with any corrections you need to make—please send your story back by e-mail. On the e-mail subject line, please state, "You have my permission to use my e-mail in your publication."

If you want to correct anything, please put your changes IN ALL CAPS. If you don't want us to use your name or those of others in your story, please tell us.

Even if you agree, we can't guarantee that our editor will accept your story. We'll let you know as soon as we receive the final word. I appreciate your considering this.

Please e-mail it to Cecil Murphey at cec.murp@ comcast.net.

You'll receive what we call a byline (your name) and one free copy of the book. If you'd like us to add your e-mail address or website so others may contact you, we'll insert those as well. Please send me your mailing address and phone number so we can send you a copy of the book when it is released in 2014.

Sorry, but for legal reasons, we have to include the next two paragraphs:

I'm writing on behalf of Don to ask you to grant permission to us, Baker Publishing Group, and their licensees, successors and assigns, to include the material indicated below in all editions and derivations of the work in all languages throughout the world and in the advertising and promotion thereof in all media now known or hereafter devised.

In agreeing, you acknowledge that you are the sole owner of the rights granted herein and that the material indicated below does not infringe upon the copyright, privacy right, or other rights of anyone.

Please print your name:

_____

Please sign your name:

_____

When Twila Belk and I wrote three compilations together, we solicited stories. For our book *I Believe in Heaven*, we included 114 stories. Some of them were from already-printed sources, which we acknowledged. But individuals who sent us a story had to sign a contract giving us permission to use their personal stories. That's becoming more and more the standard.

Before Revell released the tenth-anniversary edition of *90 Minutes in Heaven* in 2014, editor Vicki Crumpton wanted new stories. Without going into detail on how we obtained them, out of more than fifty stories Don provided for me through e-mails from readers, I narrowed it down to eleven.

I rewrote the testimonies, attempting to stay within the facts and meanings. I sent the contributors an e-mail asking for their permission. The publisher agreed to send them a copy of the book after publication. One or two asked for minor changes (and that was no problem), and all eleven of them agreed.

I kept their agreements on file because some publishers insist on having the permission forms sent to them. Other publishers, when assured that I have them, are satisfied. Vicki wanted them, so I simply forwarded all of them.

• • •

I once collaborated on a book with a gospel singer who had almost a four-octave range. In her book, she told how she had started by singing in choirs and in school and gone on to cutting records (as they did in those days). I liked working with her except for one fact: she was too candid about other people.

By that I mean, if she didn't like someone, she insisted on telling how underhanded the person was or deceptive or insensitive. She described a few times when she and another singer fought over a man and the other singer lied about my client. Despite my attempts to urge her to be a little kinder, she said, "It's the truth, and I'm going to tell the truth."

"It's your book," I said, which is my standard answer, and I meant it. My concern was that if one of those individuals named in the book chose to sue, would I be held liable for being the writer?

That happened before I signed with my first agent, so the only person I knew to ask was my editor. "What do we do?"

She didn't know, and I told her that the singer was adamant about saying what she did. "If I can't speak the truth, it's a lie," was her ultimatum. The editor said that after she received the manuscript, she'd have their on-retainer lawyer look it over.

The lawyer agreed that the singer had made a number of libelous statements. So what should we do? The lawyer dictated a short paragraph that the publisher put on the top of the copyright page: "The author assumes full responsibility for the accuracy of all facts and quotations as cited in this book."

No one ever sued, and for that I'm grateful.

Yet whenever I thought about it, I asked, "But what if they had?"

● ● ●

Another factor that comes up regularly is this: "There are people in my story who weren't nice [or whatever word they use], and they're still alive. How do I write about them?"

The answer I used to hear twenty years ago that made me chuckle when editors said it, was, "Why don't you fictionalize your story?" I wonder if they really meant those words or were trying to get out of an uncomfortable situation. I laughed because the techniques are vastly different for fiction and nonfiction. I've also read a few fictionalized manuscripts, and most of them were terrible. In fact, I can't remember one of them that read like a good novel.

The usual answer today is to change names and enough information so that the guilty won't recognize themselves.

A technique I use in my own nonfiction writing is to state in my introduction that if I used only first names, that meant I had altered people's identities to protect their privacy. If I cited first and last names, those were their actual names. This has worked for me.

The second book I did for Don Piper was with Berkley Penguin, and I used the same technique but didn't say so. When the edited version came back, the editor had changed not only the names (that had already been changed), but the genders. I explained what I had done, and that particular editor said it was routine for them because most of their writers didn't alter identities.

There is yet more to this issue. Sometimes I've heard editors and other writers say, "Wait until the person is dead before you write."

I confess, I have said it a few times as well. In my case, I'm not sure that was what I really meant or whether it was an attempt to be kind instead of saying, "This isn't a book that any publisher will buy."

I thought little about the issue until 2014, after I had finished Katariina Rosenblatt's autobiography *Stolen: The True Story of a Sex Trafficking Survivor*. We mentioned a number of things in it that, although factual, could possibly result in lawsuits. Even more serious, one of the girls that Kat had helped rescue from sex trafficking has a painful-but-poignant story. Homeland

Security has used her sworn testimony to convict several sex slavers.

The problem with her story is that the girl gave enough information that Kat later felt the perpetrators could track her down. As powerful as the story was, we deleted it because her safety was more important.

But a bigger problem faced us. How many individuals could Kat name? Some of them, such as her former husband, were crucial to the story. He refused to cooperate, which was no surprise. We had one advantage in that when they divorced, he insisted she stop using his name and go back to her maiden name of Rosenblatt.

In the book, we called him Joel and said it wasn't his real name. But that wasn't enough. I called my agent, Deidre Knight. "How do we handle this?"

She gave me exactly the answer I needed and one I hadn't heard before. "Kat has the right to tell her story." Deidre went on to explain that if we stated the events as her recollection or understanding, Kat wasn't stating facts, only opinion.

During the years Kat was involved in sex trafficking, her traffickers kept her controlled by giving her all the cocaine she wanted. So one of the things we said in the book was that cocaine had destroyed parts of her memory and that this was her best recall of the events.

Perhaps three times in the book, we made statements to that effect, and one of those statements involved her former husband. After we did that, Vicki Crumpton showed it to their lawyer, who approved. The book is now in print exactly that way.

The point of the account above is to say that people *can* tell their stories and they can name the guilty—but they can't do it as fact or accusation. By authors saying that this is the way they understood or perceived a situation, it becomes opinion and not fact.

• • •

When I began to write about the physical and sexual abuse of my childhood, my perpetrators were dead. My first perpetrator, a female relative, had been dead for two decades, but her children and grandchildren were alive. I didn't feel it was my responsibility to inform them about what she had done to me. Therefore, I called her a female relative—which was true—without identifying her.

Although some write memoirs and autobiographies to vindicate themselves or point fingers, I've never felt right about doing that and have turned down several lucrative book offers that seemed to be about revenge.

The second question I hear then (or sometimes later) is, "But what if other family members [or friends or neighbors] remember the incidents differently?" The answer is, "Count on it that they will." So how do you handle it?

The rule is that you have the right to tell your story from your own personal, subjective point of view. We all tend to remember incidents differently. As long as you stay within the subjective voice ("This is how I remember") and not the objective ("This is exactly what happened"), you can expect no problems.

TAKEAWAYS

- You can be sued, but you can also protect yourself.
- Whenever you use real names and situations, get those individuals to sign a permission form.
- If the author insists on making strong statements as fact, you can ask the publishers to state on the copyright page, "The author assumes full responsibility for the accuracy of all facts and quotations as cited in this book."
- If you can't get permission or choose not to do so, disguise people's names, genders, or locations so that the information remains true but the people can't identify themselves.
- The author does have the right to tell her story. But you need to make it clear that it's the author's opinion or don't state the information as fact.

24

WHY DO YOU NEED A
LITERARY AGENT?

The most obvious reason a writer needs an agent is that today, except with small publishers, agents are clearing houses for publishers. They take 15 percent off the top of the royalty payments, and they provide invaluable service.

Good agents not only link you with publishers, they earn their percentage by standing up for your rights. If you as the writer ask the publisher for a higher advance, a larger royalty rate, or more copies, you may come across as greedy and difficult to deal with.

As for me, I like not having to talk about money, and I don't like having to read through contracts—filled with a lot of legalese. Agents do the tedious legal and accounting work and catch things you would never notice.

The first contract my present agent received with an offer from a medium-sized publisher was so bad that she not only negotiated it, she showed them how to improve their contracts. To their credit, the publishing house made those changes permanent.

Only a few times in my years of professional writing have I had issues with the editor. In those cases, I notified my agent and she stood with me. As far as I can remember, we always won those issues.

The best quality I like about my agent is the freedom I have to throw a book idea at her and get her feedback. Twice I had ideas that I was certain would sell—and was ready to start work on them. But just to be sure, I e-mailed Deidre, and she told me why she couldn't sell such a book. I trusted her instincts and declined.

On the other hand, Katariina Rosenblatt, a survivor of sex trafficking, came to me, saying she'd like me to write her book for her. I was hesitant, mainly because I knew nothing about the drug culture or that nether world of trafficking in human lives. I wasn't sure the book would sell. At least that was my approach to my agent.

Deidre pushed right through my hesitation, assured me that it was becoming a hot topic, and said, "You can do it." I hadn't said I was anxious about it, but she picked up on that. That's another reason I'm grateful for my agent—her sensitivity to my situation.

• • •

As a collaborator, when do you try to get an agent?

Too many writers reach out before they have a good, finished product. But if you feel you've written a good book and are confident it's the best you can do, then go for it.

To that I would also add, before you send it on, let a professional editor look at the manuscript. (If you're an editor, my advice is still the same.) If you can't afford to pay for the entire manuscript, at least hire someone to do the first three chapters. When those chapters come back, look at them as objectively as you can, and learn from what she said.

And that raises the next question, how do you get a good freelance editor? Ask other writers. Go online. But be careful. Because I write primarily for the inspirational-Christian market, two helpful websites are www.thechristianpen.com or www.christiancommunicator.com. There are other such groups you can contact.

In trying to get a literary agent to accept you as a client, find out who the agents are who work in your field. Go to the Web. Chuck Sambuchino publishes an annual *Guide of Literary Agents: The Most Trusted Guide to Getting Published.* You can find more information in *The Christian Writer's Market Guide*, an annual publication in print but also kept up-to-date online at christianwritersmarketguide.com.

Your job will be to prove that you are worth an agent's time. Or to put it more crassly, can an agent make money representing you?

Look up prospective agents' websites. They list their guidelines for clients. Consider those guidelines as *commands*, and follow them closely. Your ability to do so will tell an agent the kind of person you are.

Before you contact an agent, check out his name online. If there are questions about that person's ethics, someone will report it.

You might ask if the agent is a member of the Association of Authors' Representatives—which functions as a self-policing agency.

Another significant thing you can do to attract a literary agent is attend writers conferences, which I've also mentioned elsewhere. Check out the conferences online, and read the list of the faculty members. If they have editors and agents, that means you can make appointments with them (usually fifteen minutes) as part of your conference fee. Many conferences offer a paid critique service, and you pay for thirty minutes with an editor or another writer who has read your proposal or sample chapter. You can usually designate the person you want. The rates change over time, but at one conference I recently attended, the conferees paid $30.

To this matter of appointments, agent Terry Burns of the Hartline Literary Agency once wrote,[18]

> First, fifteen-minute appointments aren't long enough to sell your book. Most agents and editors will tell you they have seldom if ever made a decision about a project while at a conference. I think I have done it twice. However, it is enough time to generate our interest in a proposal and create a favorable impression so we will remember you when that proposal arrives.
>
> Second, make a good, brief pitch and then shut up. Those who spend the whole time talking tend not to engage the interest of those they are meeting with. Allow the agent or editor to ask questions about things he wants to know so he can gauge his level of interest. The target is a dialogue or exchange, not a lecture.
>
> Finally, it's good to have a one sheet and/or a proposal with you, but be aware that most of those

---

18   Terry Burns, twburns@suddenlink.net.

you meet with do not want to take hard copy material with them. But like the Boy Scout motto says, "Be prepared." Occasionally there may be that person who wants to read something while they're there or on the airplane home and will select your proposal for that purpose.

You are there to impart *and receive* information. Impart enough to pave the way for the proposal you will probably be invited to send, and receive about the interest of the person you are meeting with that you can reference in your cover letter to personalize it.

• • •

If an *agent* wants to see your book, wait until after the conference, and e-mail it as an attachment. In the subject line write, "Requested Material, XXX Writers Conference." The agent will remember you.

If an *editor* wants to see your proposal or manuscript, do the same thing. If you are offered a contract, before you sign it, contact an agent that you would like to represent you and say, "XX Publishers has offered me a contract. Would you be willing to represent me?"

If the agent agrees, she'll negotiate for you. It also makes the agent aware of you, and possibly you'll receive ongoing representation.

Although it may be difficult to sign with an agent, once you sign, the agent works for you. Never forget that if the agent asks for money, cut off the contact. Reputable agents rely on commissions (royalties) from selling books.

Takeaways

- You need a literary agent to market your manuscripts, unless you choose to self-publish or aim at a small publisher that doesn't require an agent.
- Most publishers won't look at anything not submitted by a literary agent.
- Agents get you better deals than you can make for yourself.
- Good agents function as your advisor or sounding board.
- Agents do the tedious legal and accounting work and catch things you would never notice.
- Agents know the business and have a large number of contacts with editors and publishing houses.
- In case of conflict, your agent functions as an intermediary between you and the author and with the publishing house.
- Your agent can be a source of new clients for you.

How do you get a literary agent?
- Learn about agents and what kind of books they handle.
- Go to websites of agents and see what they want from prospective clients.
- Attend conferences and make appointments with agents and editors.
- At the conference, talk to other writers about agents. Those with either very good or very bad reputations are widely known.

25

LET'S TALK MONEY

The most common question from new ghostwriters is, quite naturally, how much should I charge?

Before I answer, I'll start with explaining how authors and publishers pay collaborators. I've made a comfortable living as a collaborator. Unless the writer does the work gratis—and no professional does that—there are three ways you are paid.

1. Flat fee. As the term implies, it means you receive a specific amount of money for writing the book and nothing else. When writing for a flat fee, some publishers offer writers a particular amount if the collaborators' names are on the cover and a larger amount if they write it without credit.

Sometimes writers and publishers call the flat fee a work-for-hire agreement, which I did until my editor friend Steven Lawson corrected me.

Here's a rather tedious explanation of the term *work-for-hire*. A Supreme Court decision in the case of CCNV versus Reid concluded that Congress provides two distinct means for classifying projects as work-for-hire. The first concerns work created by employees within the scope of their employment in which the copyright belongs to the employer.

The second section of the law requires that three conditions must exist to designate a work-for-hire: the work must be (1) specially ordered or commissioned; (2) both parties must sign a written document in which they agree that the book is a work-for-hire; and (3) the work must be for use as a contribution to a collective work, part of a motion picture or other audiovisual work, a translation, a supplementary work and compilation, instructional text, a test, answer material for a test, or an atlas.

The term is so common in publishing that most professionals don't know the difference between it and a flat fee. But you know.

When the book is a flat-fee project, the person who assigns the work owns all rights.

The duration of the copyright in a work made for hire or a flat-fee project lasts for seventy-five years from the year of its first publication, or one hundred years from its creation. On all other works, the copyright law of 1978, says it's valid for the life of the last surviving author plus seventy years.

2. Royalty payments. The original idea was that patrons sponsored promising authors, poets, musicians, and artists by supporting them so they could devote themselves to their work. That agreement functioned much like the modern grant.

That's also from the historical era, from which we get the term *freelance*. Sir Walter Scott's novel *Ivanhoe* (1820) described a medieval mercenary warrior as being "free lance," supposedly the first mention in English. That meant the fighter wasn't sworn to the service of anyone, and his weapon—the lance—was available for hire.

About forty years later the term changed to a figurative meaning and became recognized as a verb in the early 1900s. The meaning turned from a noun (a freelance) to an adjective (freelance journalist) about fifty years after that.

Royalty rates for electronic books are still in flux, so I don't have any information, except to say they are considerably higher than for hard copy books. The figure I hear most often is 25 percent of the sale price.

Most general-market houses pay royalty on the retail (what consumers pay), and Christian publishers pay a slightly higher rate based on the net (or wholesale rate).

As a general rule, New York houses pay 10 percent royalty on the retail price of a hardback. That is, if readers pay $20, the author receives $2.

By contrast, Christian publishers will pay about 14 percent based on the wholesale price which is usually half the retail. Thus writers will receive $1.40 on a book that wholesales for $10 and retails for $20.

Below is a chart comparing the differences. Although the rates of 20 percent don't hold true, the principle is correct.[19]

Book-Publishing Royalties
"Net" and "Retail" Compared

	Retail Basis	Net Basis
Cover Price	$15.00	$15.00
Discount to Booksellers	50%	50%
Wholesale Price	$7.50	$7.50
Printing Cost (200-Page Book)	$3.50	$3.50
Net Income	$4.00	$4.00
Royalty Rate	20%	20%
Royalty Calculation	0.20x15	0.20x4
Royalty	$3.00	$0.80

---

19   http://en.wikipedia.org/wiki/Royalties.

I prefer to work on royalty, even though I could cite instances in which I would have made more money asking for a flat fee. I chose the royalty method so I could have a stake in the sales of those books. I wanted them to succeed. Of course, I want every book I write to do well, but a royalty payment gives me a sense of ownership in the writing.

3. Flat fee plus royalty. This is rarely offered. I agreed to this only once, and the book did well, but not well enough to make a difference. It sold seventy-five thousand copies, and only after it hit one hundred thousand would I have received any additional funds.

Literary agent Steven Hutson writes, "Royalties are a bit of a gamble for the writer. We like to suggest a combination of fee plus a small percentage. That is not always possible to achieve."[20]

• • •

Now that I've given the basics, how much do you charge for ghostwriting? The two ways I see most are:

1. Charging by the hour (sometimes by the page). This method works for writers, but authors are sometimes hesitant because they don't know the final cost.

2. Charging a flat fee. This is one price (plus travel expenses). It's easy and clear.

In the early years of my freelance career, I charged by the hour (and I'm a fast writer). When I was still transcribing my own material, I included that expense in my hourly pricing.

That leads us back to the question, "How much money?"

That's not easy to explain, but I'll try.

---

20   Steven Hutson, literary agent, www.wordwisemedia.com.

The most accurate answer is this: it depends. Let's start with how collaborators receive their work.

1. Client initiative. This is the usual pattern for me. Don Piper approached me to write *90 Minutes in Heaven*. Katariina Rosenblatt did as well for her book *Stolen*. When that happens, we have to explain our fees.

Please notice that unless the authors want to self-publish, we start with a book proposal. If you're ready to become a ghostwriter, part of your preparation is to be familiar with writing proposals, so I don't discuss the how-to steps.

Sometimes the book doesn't sell, so the author decides to self-publish, and that constitutes a different arrangement, which usually means a new contract.

So how much do you charge to write a book proposal?

Again, the answer is, "It depends." I vaguely recall reading a statistic that said the range went from $5,000 to $100,000 and the average was $36,000. That's a wide range. I also know two experienced writers who charge only $2,500.

Here's how I answer: your price depends on what you feel you can ask. I see this as a question of self-worth. In my early days, my rates were low ($1,000), but with each sale, I grew more comfortable asking for more. Today I have a range that depends on the scope of the book and the likelihood of it being sold. My lowest figure is $6,000.

The next question is, if I accept money for the proposal and the book doesn't sell, do I have to return the money? The answer is no.

For many years, if the book sold, I refunded the money I'd received from my portion of the advance. If the figure that had been paid to me was less than the money I received from the advance, I paid the author my total portion of the advance, and the contract was finished. I refused to start a book in debt.

I no longer operate that way. These days the money authors pay me for writing the proposal is nonrefundable. I made that decision after several editors pointed out that the ghostwriters they worked with kept money as payment for the proposal, whether the book sold or not.

I decided they were correct. Writing good proposals is a lot of work. Mine run thirty-five to seventy-five pages and include up to three chapters of the book.

If I move on to a flat-rate project, which I rarely do, I charge anywhere from $30,000 to $50,000 for a book. A few highly experienced ghostwriters ask for $85,000 and above.

One writer friend ghosted his first book and couldn't sell it to a royalty-paying publisher, and later the author decided to self-publish. About that time I offered to pass a flat-fee project on to him and asked his price.

"I want $25,000."

I laughed. "You're not experienced enough for that amount." He replied that an agent had told him that was the going rate.

"Maybe for experienced writers, but you don't have the credentials." That was the last communication we had.

Most of the people among whom I mingle start a flat-fee project at $5,000 to $7,500 for their first book, and occasionally $10,000. After that, much depends on their experience and the success of their projects.

Or as I often tell beginners, it depends on your sense of self-worth. Ask for a fee or a rate at which you're comfortable. As someone said recently, "This is a slow-building career. You start low and increase your prices as you count your successes."

Just to be clear about myself, I work on a royalty percent—50 percent of the royalty. That's standard for experienced ghostwriters and collaborators. However, when I decided to work on royalty, I started with only 35 percent, then went to 40, and now it's strictly 50 percent.

2. The publisher contacts you. Usually this is because you've worked with them previously, someone has referred you to them, or they simply know of your achievements. I prefer this approach because the finances are fairly well settled, and the editor negotiates with my agent. My book *Bloodline: The John Turnipseed Story* began with an e-mail from a man I liked and had worked with before in a different publishing house. I referred him to my agent, and the two of them negotiated a nice advance and royalty rates.

3. The writer initiates. I have not taken the initiative. Ever. In the first days of my ghosting career, I promised God and myself that I wouldn't seek clients. "If you want me to write their books, they have to come to me."

I don't suggest this is the route for anyone else, but it was the right decision for me. I've made a good living for more than thirty years. And since the success of *90 Minutes in Heaven*, I've turned away more authors than I've accepted.

4. Ghostwriting services. Some collaborators offer themselves through ghostwriting services. Twice such companies called to recruit me, and I have no idea how they got my name.

The first company called me in 1996. Although they didn't disclose what they charged their clients, they offered me a flat fee of $75,000 to write a book. It was a nice amount of money, and they set up a conference call, but I wasn't allowed to know the client's full name or address. During the half-hour conversation, the author explained the basis for his book. I didn't feel comfortable with his ideas for a book and didn't think it was theologically sound, so I turned them down.

About a year later someone from a second agency called. I heard what kind of book they wanted, and before they talked money, I told them I wasn't interested. I wanted to select my own clients and meet them in person.

If you're interested in signing with such an agency, check the Internet. I found several under "Ghostwriting Services."

• • •

Now we're ready to answer the question, "How do you decide on your fees?"

There are no written guidelines about what you can or should charge. After discussing this matter with other writers, I've listed below how some of them decide on the amount they charge.

Please realize that ghostwriting consists of far more than writing books for someone else. It also includes writing articles, newsletters, promotional pieces, or anything else in print, but I'll limit the scope to books.

One agent has several collaborators under contract and pays them a flat fee of $5,000, which I think is cheap and disrespectful of their talent.

I suggest that if you start moving into this field, ask other writers what they charge. Check online. Most of the writers I know are willing to tell you how they price their writing. You can also find websites that show standard rates for various types of writing and editing services. Values change regularly, so the figures I use may not be valid when you read this.

If you have a publishing record or significant expertise in a field such as law or medicine, make a point of mentioning that when you consult with possible authors. They pay for your experience and knowledge as well as your writing skills.

Although I wrote my first ghostwriting project in 1982, it wasn't until 1984 that I began ghostwriting full time. I started my full-time freelance career by charging $35 an hour because I work fast, and it only took me a couple of books to figure out that I was undercharging. I raised my hourly rate several times. I finally figured out that I needed to make $100 an hour to feel that the work was worthwhile.

As soon as I mentioned that number, authors resisted, so I figured out a different approach. Aside from the fact that $100 seems too expensive, another factor was the most pressing question of authors: "What's the total cost?" That was reasonable, and I wanted to give them a clear answer.

After that, when I met with prospects, I heard their pitch about what they wanted. As they talked, I mentally calculated how long it would take. A few I could do in three months, and others might take twice that time. But the average was four months. (To be able to figure that out probably means you will need some previous experience in actually writing for someone else.)

"I estimate that it will take me about four months to write your book," I told them. I mentioned the amount of money I wanted to make in one calendar year. "So I will charge you one-third of my annual income to write your book, and you'll receive my full-time services."

They seemed to understand a firm figure. In those days I absorbed the cost of long-distance phone calls, paper and printing, and transcription. If it involved travel, the clients paid for that as well as my expenses while with them, and that hasn't changed.

• • •

As I point out elsewhere, pricing is a highly individual matter. Before you set your rates, I want to point out a few things to take into consideration. I asked several writers how much they charged for ghostwriting. Some of them do what I call book doctoring and consider it ghostwriting. A book doctor takes material given by the author and reshapes it to make it readable. For me, the distinction is that if the author submits written text (or even sermons or lectures) for the writer to rewrite, that's usually the function of a book doctor.

Many professional ghostwriters cite hourly prices, which indicates that they started with some kind of written or recorded material.

For the rest of this chapter, I'll assume that you start with nothing and will write the entire manuscript.

How many revisions are you willing to write before the author pays extra? And if you charge, how much? Write that figure into the contract. If you're not willing to stay at a manuscript for as many revisions as it takes, you need to make that clear.

I've never set a number of revisions. I'm willing to make as many as the authors want. So far I've had only one demanding client who refused to do any work on his own and forced me to go through three sessions where he read the manuscript aloud in my presence and made changes on the spot.

All my other clients have worked on the manuscripts after I've sent them, made corrections, and returned them. I smooth out the changes and send them back for a second round. If there are still issues, I'm willing to keep at it.

Before you start, learn everything you can about the project and the client. As I point out elsewhere, for professional writers there is always some research. No matter how much material you receive from the author, you will need to verify dates, check facts, and cite references. Because you're a professional, never assume you know. Especially check quotations by the famous. These days you can locate the source of almost any quotation on the Internet.

Is it a topic with which you're familiar? If not, how much will it demand of you to become familiar with it? If you're writing a personal experience, you'll have the opportunity to ask questions during your sessions. But if you write in the field of medicine, for example, you might do preliminary research so you know something about the line of work.

How often does the client want to hear from you? How often do you want to hear from the author? Although I answered this in a previous chapter, it's significant in deciding on your price.

You want to know the person's expectations. And the author needs to know your preferences. One client I had seemed to want to talk every day "so we can both stay close to the material." And the calls usually lasted close to an hour. I told her that if she insisted on that arrangement, it would take at least twice the time to do the work.

I told her that I get into what I call the writing zone, and whenever I'm interrupted, I have to backtrack to pick up my thoughts and start zoning in again. "I prefer infrequent calls and only in the case of something relevant."

I did add, "If you feel you need to check in every week, please make it Saturday afternoon when I don't work."

She got the message, and we had a good working relationship.

Do you have an editor to work behind you? Everyone—without exception—needs an editor. Include that as part of your hidden cost. No matter how careful you are, you don't see your own typos or repetition of words.

What is the deadline? Does the author have a specific date in mind? If so, don't agree to it unless you're positive you can meet it. Even if you think you can, something such as illness or family emergencies could prevent your doing the work on time. If this happens, immediately notify the author of the situation and explain when you anticipate finishing—and give as early a date as you can reasonably estimate.

I usually build in a little more time than I feel I need for two reasons. And by "a little more time," I mean one month.

First, the obvious reason is that if something unexpected disrupts my life, I can cope and still meet my deadline. Second, is a psychological factor. If I promise the author, "I'll have this to you by April 10," and I finish four weeks early, I can honestly say, "I got so involved in this project, I completed it earlier than I had projected."

Be clear about ownership of the material and the byline on the book. Normally the author owns the copyright. For you as a writer, that's not significant. In effect, it shows their ownership, which is as it should be.

• • •

In preparing this, I contacted a number of professionals in the publishing industry, and here are their responses.

The Editorial Freelancers Association charges $50 to $60 an hour or $0.26 to $0.50 a word. My assumption is that that's a rate for what I'd term book doctoring.[21]

Jeanne Marie Leach, whose fees are probably for articles or book doctoring, says, "Most of my collaborating and ghostwriting jobs have come through the Christian Editor Connection. You must become a member to receive leads. The latest ghostwriting job I got came from Thumbtack.com. You pay per bid. Anything I want to bid on comes with a cost of approximately $6.35. I paid $75 and ended up with two smaller projects for $400 each and one *excellent* ghostwriting job. This client has a three-book series for me to write. Once I finish with these projects, I will definitely go back to Thumbtack for more business."

Brenda Kay Coulter stated regarding her projects, "I'm currently changing $500 down and $30 an hour.[22]

Donna Schlachter declined to list the amount of money but sent this information:

> When I did the work-for-hire books, the publisher set the amount they would pay, which was paid over three installments—25 percent at contract signing, 50 percent at submission of final manuscript, and the final 25 percent at acceptance of final manuscript.
>
> For the ghostwriting contract I did for a nonfiction book, I tried to estimate how many hours it was going to take me, including research, time with the author, reading her journals, coming up with the chapter

---

21   http://www.the-efa.org/res/rates.php.

22   Brenda Kay Coulter, bkcoulter@sbcglobal.net.

outlines, writing, and editing, and I multiplied that by my hourly rate. Then I gave the author the option of paying me up front with the understanding that if either of us canceled the contract before the book was finished, she would pay a premium rate (higher than the total cost divided by the estimated number of pages) per page for what had already been written and I would refund her the balance; or she could pay as I submitted each section, usually three chapters at a time, with no refund once the pages were written, as the money was considered earned. We estimated how many pages the book would be based on the chapter outlines.

We also checked online at various ghostwriting sites to see if my price was in line with the market, and the author seemed pleased with the price, so we felt that was a confirmation.[23]

Another ghostwriter, who asked not to be identified because she plans to increase her rates, stated that she received $5,000 to prepare a book proposal and $15,000 for writing the book. If it's a rush job, she charges $20,000 to $25,000.

Another wrote, "I use my ghostwriting as a ministry for people who can't afford the normal rate, so my charge is $5,000 for the first one hundred pages and then $3,000 for each one hundred pages after that. If they cannot afford that, I offer royalty options."

Sally Hanan writes, "I'm working on my first ghostwriting job. The client has already written the book, so I already have

---

23   Donna Schlachter, op. cit.

all the facts and timeline in place. I'm charging her $35 an hour, but if I had to work from scratch, I'd ask for $50."

Since 1985, Susan Osborn has been in business offering the full range of writing and editing services. She employs a staff of eighteen editors. Specifically I asked her about book doctoring. "We charge $40 an hour."[24]

Agent Steven Hutson responds from the perspective of a literary agency looking for writers: "There are several factors. What's the writer's going rate? If it's too high, we'll have to consider someone else. How difficult will the project be to write? Is it a hard topic to write on? Is the author tricky to work with? What's the availability of the writer? Usually we want to get started right away, and that's not always possible given the writer's current workload. Is the writer local? Local is often an advantage, although these days it shouldn't be."[25]

Steven goes on to talk about the pricing. "The answer, as you can imagine, is highly nuanced. It depends on (1) the budget for the project. If funded by the principal (the celebrity or the author), that is one thing. If it is funded by the publisher, that is another. (2) The market reach for the project. If a book is to be self-published, it is unlikely a ghost or collaborator can charge $50,000 and still sleep at night with integrity intact. But undercharging can be a crime too.

"We've had people complain that paying $5,000 is too much for a collaborator. But we've also had people complain that $25,000 is too much. I even complained on behalf of a client when a collaborator quoted a fee of $75,000 for their participation."

---

24   Susanosb@aol.com or www.christiancommunicator.com.

25   Steve Hutson, op. cit.

• • •

Above I mentioned copyright, so let's be clear. Copyright refers to protection of what we call intellectual property rights of the material. Copyright protects the author. You do not need to apply for a copyright unless the author is self-publishing and doing everything from getting ISBN numbers to hiring printers and graphic artists. If the author chooses to self-publish, established self-publishing companies provide everything needed in their contract, which includes copyright information.

The law doesn't copyright titles or ideas, only the written expressions, which means that when you have their material in what we refer to as a fixed form, it's protected by common law.

Please don't use the copyright symbol. If you send your material to an agent or a royalty publisher, to use the © implies that you don't trust them and want to warn them that they can't steal from you.

Another way to say it is that the © is one of the marks of an amateur. If you have any questions about copyright laws, the Internet has any number of sites with answers.

Copyright infringement is punishable by law and occurs when anyone uses, copies, or distributes a copyrighted work without the permission of the copyright owner.

You do need to be aware of what we call *fair use*.[26] The problem is that it's difficult to define the term. If you quote from the Bible, on the copyright page of a translation, you can learn how many words or verses you can use without writing for permission.

---

26   http://copyright.laws.com/what-is-copyright#sthash.g7h4QKAh.dpuf. This is one of several sites.

Some publishing houses allow 250 words and others 500. It's your responsibility to find out their word limits *and* cite every source you quote. Be aware that poetry and music laws are strict. Even a dozen words of a song can cost you money—a lot of money.

That means that whenever you forward jokes or poignant pieces without the author's permission, you violate the copyright of the author.

The current copyright law says that anything published *after* 1923 is protected by copyright. So if you quote from any publication earlier than 1923, cite the reference and add the words *in the public domain*.

TAKEAWAYS

- As a ghostwriter, you earn money by flat fees, royalty, or (rarely) flat fee plus royalty.
- You receive collaborative work four ways: the client initiates; the publisher approaches you; you seek clients; you work through a ghostwriting service.
- You have to set your own fees, and those fees depend on your own sense of self-worth as a ghostwriter. You can check with others who do this work, but if you're beginning, don't expect the higher rate.

26

THE GHOSTWRITING PROCESS

Here are a few points I want to emphasize if you continue to explore becoming a collaborator.

Authors hire professionals to help them get a book written. "Help them" really means ghostwriters usually write every word, subject to correction or clarification by the author.

If you're already a professional writer, writing is *your job*; it's what you do. You like it, and you're good at it. It doesn't overwhelm you to sit in front of a blank computer terminal and come up with a first sentence. And you follow that with many paragraphs and pages.

If you're not a professional writer, this theoretically simple task can be as overwhelming as handing a writer a scalpel and saying, "Okay, make your first cut."

Although I've covered some of this in previous chapters, I want to emphasize the following points.

1. Listen to the person speaking so you get her tone, her inflection, her word choices, and her take on life ingrained into your writing for the project.

2. Always do in-person interviews when possible. Even if a full interview isn't scheduled, consider a meeting to get to know the person better. Offer to meet the author on his turf. Seeing someone in his home or personal office can be revealing and give you insights you'd never get if you met on neutral territory.

3. Pretend you're a dummy and the author is the ventriloquist. Ideally you will convey through the words you type what the ventriloquist speaks in the manner and style in which he speaks. You will be presenting the author in such a way that others who read the work will not know he didn't write it. I'd say that's the highest compliment a ghostwriter can get.

A friend told me that she once wrote a small booklet for the senior pastor of the mega-church she attended. After she handed it to him, he read it, smiled his approval, and said, "Sounds just like me."

That meant she did such a good job of capturing his voice and personality that he was pleased.

4. Carefully heed the author's feedback. If she says, "This doesn't sound like me," or, "I wouldn't say it that way," your answer is always, "I'll fix it." And you will, because the author is the owner of the work and has to stand up for and defend anything in the book.

5. If you can't settle your differences, go to your agent or the publisher. If there's only you and the author, you have to decide if you can live with what the author wants. If you can't, break the contract. (This is why I always include an escape clause.)

• • •

I get along with editors, and that's not true with every writer. Instead of being convinced that they're trying to ruin my marvelous prose, I work on the premise that they want to improve the quality and make the work a top-selling book.

Editing is what I call a give-and-take process. Some writers don't realize that the editors' reputations at the publishing houses are involved. If a book gets bad reviews because of grammatical errors, for instance, it reflects on them.

I can cite one exception by an editor, whose editing was so bad that I appealed to the publisher, who agreed and gave me someone else. My original opening began: "Prayer sometimes bores me and I wonder why I do it; sometimes prayer excites me and I *know* why I do it."

She said that kind of language belonged in a journal and not in a trade book. She revised it to say, "Prayer, at its best, is an intimate conversation with God."

Can you see why I objected?

That was the exception. Truly professional editors want the book to succeed, and they want it to sound as much like the author as possible.

• • •

To prepare yourself for ghostwriting projects, below are my suggestions:
- Be convinced that you want to do the project.
- Remind yourself of the time and commitment it will take for you to write the book, especially if you can't write full time.
- Decide on the place for the interview. If you travel, the author pays for your transportation.

- Be sure your recording equipment is in working condition.
- Try to be open with the client by asking questions that force him to think deeply. Aim for answers that will touch readers.
- Encourage the author to tell you stories and anecdotes. An easy way to do that is to say, "Give me an example," or, "Tell me when you faced such a situation."
- Don't be afraid of your author's tears or anger unless they're directed at you. Take them as a sign of trust in you.
- Provide the author with various drafts of the material so she can make changes.

Once you turn in the book as a completed project, think of it as just that: completed. From the beginning, get used to saying to the author, "Your book." You need to remove any sense of ownership. You get paid for your work, and you release ownership.

TAKEAWAYS

- Listen to the person speaking so you get his tone, inflection, and word choices.
- Always do in-person interviews when possible.
- Pretend you're the dummy and the author is the ventriloquist. Ideally you will convey through the words you pen what the ventriloquist speaks in the manner and style in which she speaks.
- Carefully heed the author's feedback.
- If you can't settle your differences, get out of the contract.

27

MY GHOSTWRITING PROCESS

This probably isn't how others do it, but this is the Murphey method of ghostwriting and the sequential steps I go through on collaborative projects.

1. The preliminary contact and an in-person meeting must come first. To prepare for that, I look up the individual on the Internet, if there are any links on her, so I can be informed on who she is and what she's done.

2. We meet and talk, and *if we like each other*, we move forward. If we don't, either of us can say no.

3. If I say yes, I ask for resources to make me better prepared.

4. At an agreed-on date, we meet again, and I conduct the interviews. I tape everything digitally, download it on Dropbox (or a similar site), and send the link to my transcriber.

Some people use voice-recognition software such as Dragon NaturallySpeaking. I tried it once and found it difficult with two different voices. Others may disagree.

5. After having the digital recording transcribed, I organize the material. And the taped transcripts often run 250 to 300 pages. For me, the organizing takes at least a week.

When authors speak, I don't try to censor them or redirect unless they stray badly. Often they'll talk and then say, "Oh, yes, that reminds me . . ." and they tell a story that fits somewhere else. Or there's a connection, and I need to figure it out.

I go over the material and decide the order that fits best with the type of book. I devise a preliminary outline as well as one or two sentences to explain each chapter.

6. Just before I write the proposal, I ask for a resume, which I rewrite using bullets. Occasionally I find and suggest endorsers or marketing opportunities through his contacts—something he doesn't think about. I ask him for possible endorsers and, when it seems appropriate, someone to write the foreword for the book.

As I write the proposal, I include a marketing plan. If she has any ideas beyond what I write, this is the time for her to let me know.

As I look for competing books, I rely on the author for help if the book is other than an autobiography. For example, when I wrote *Live 10 Healthy Years Longer* with Dr. Jan Kuzma, I asked him for books in the field so that I could compare and write an annotated bibliography. Jan was an expert in nutrition and health and certainly knew the field better than I did.

7. After I complete the book proposals, I send them to authors and ask them to put any changes in **bold** so I don't miss corrections.

For a time, I tried to teach the authors to use comment

boxes, and a few either couldn't seem to stay with it or were frustrated. It seemed easier for them to write in the text itself.

If I don't agree with any of their suggested changes, I explain the reason to them. I can't think of an incident in which the revisions have been a serious problem. My position remains: the author has the final word on content.

8. I send back the corrected proposal to make sure I've gotten everything and give authors another opportunity to add or make changes.

9. Once the author is satisfied, I send the proposal to my agent with a copy to the author. Sometimes Deidre suggests changes. I make them and return the corrected manuscript to her and the author.

10. Once Deidre is satisfied, she decides on a list of publishing houses that she thinks would be open to the book.

It's a slow, deliberate pondering, and she usually ends up with ten to fifteen publishers. She sends me a list with the names of the publishers and editors. As she receives responses, she either forwards the editor's e-mail or simply tells me, "HarperCollins passed." Usually I'm the one who informs the author.

Typically, I don't notify the author about each rejection—he gets discouraged. And the first responses are usually the ones that say, "Thanks, but this isn't a book for us."

Please notice that unless my agent already represents the author, she deals only with me until we sell the book.

On rare occasions, my agent goes to a book auction. That means she believes there's a high level of interest and the book will bring in a large advance and a higher level of royalty.

Again, Deidre makes out her list and contacts the publishers. She tells them when the bids are due. I'm not sure why, but every bid I've known about closes at noon on a Wednesday, and it's usually for a thirty-day period.

Although some agents do, Deidre doesn't include the low ceiling, meaning the bids *start* at a certain level.

My agent has done this only three times for books I've sent, and it's been quite an experience. After the success of *90 Minutes in Heaven,* she auctioned a three-book follow up, which Berkley/Penguin won.

11. Aside from the auction, as a general rule, after Deidre sends on the proposal, the first few days we get passes from those who have no interest in the book. Sometimes the acceptance comes immediately, and that's always exciting.

12. Then comes the waiting period—sometimes two or three months after she sends out a proposal.

13. Under normal conditions, I work on something else while I wait. My position is that if the book doesn't sell, which happens, I haven't wasted time. I usually have other projects. I send out two twice-weekly blog posts, and I often write two or three months of columns during those slow times. Sometimes I travel and speak.

14. We receive an offer. Sometimes more than one, which is quite nice. This is where the author comes into the action. Then all three of us discuss the terms and decide which to accept.

I can't think of any instance in which my agent has suggested one publisher and the author and I have disagreed. She is the professional in her area, and that's why we hire her.

15. All three of us agree with the publisher on all the pertinent factors, including the due date and the word count. Supposedly, the first part of the advance is paid "on signing the contract," which really means about sixty days *after* the publisher receives the signed contract.

The contract stipulates the number of free copies we receive—and that varies with publishers. They also tell us what it will cost us to buy copies. If we buy copies, which figure into the number sold, they don't count when computing royalties.

In the contract stage the author is then handed over to Deidre for that book.

16. I don't wait for the check to arrive but go to work on finishing the book immediately. I read through the material again to refresh my memory. And that's important, because new ideas or approaches become clear during that fallow period. I work long hours for five and a half days a week until I complete the draft.

17. My focus is to tell a coherent story or write a logical outline as I write the first full draft of the manuscript. And in doing that, I aim for incorporating the authors' voices and personalities. That's become easier over the years, because I immerse myself in listening to them. I try not to use words and phrases the authors wouldn't find natural.

My first drafts aren't what I call pretty. I don't get too concerned over syntax because I don't want to slow down the process to focus on grammar or verb tense. I don't try to polish the prose until I've gotten feedback and know it's all right to proceed.

18. Usually, I send the full manuscript to the author twice for changes. After that, it's normally only a sentence or two, but I stay at it until the author says, "Yes, it's finished." This is the author's book, and I want to satisfy her (even though sometimes I wonder if I'll ever do that). Some authors become obsessed and keep changing and changing. That's especially true with first-time authors. Sometimes I have to write and ask them to let it go and move on.

The late Norman Vaughn was the worst for adding anecdotes. He kept wanting to include more stories—all of them were excellent, but not all of them fit the scope of the book. On our first book, four or five times I tried to get him to realize we didn't need more. "We have enough stories. We've met our word count and can't keep adding new material."

Norman was such a lovable man that it was difficult to get upset with him, and the stories were absolutely delightful. But he couldn't seem to stop.

Finally, I called the editor and said, "If you want this book done on time and within the word count you asked for, *you* have to tell Norman to stop adding material."

She did, and he sent *her* more stories, but she told him, "We've already exceeded the word limit" (which was true).

19. And last, I send the final draft to the publisher with a copy to the author. And I move on to new projects.

20. Months later, both the author and I receive an edited version of the manuscript as an e-mail attachment using track changes. Increasingly publishers are using pdf. The comments are what I call broad-brush editing. That is, it deals with the substance and overview. I respond to the revisions and send my copy on to the author.

If there are specific questions for the author, I make sure my client takes note. For instance, the editor may ask questions about a date or the spelling of a name, and I must defer to the author.

The publishing house usually gives us a week—which is sometimes a rush. Sometimes they give us two weeks. One time the author wasn't available and I needed to get his response to three questions, so the editor gave me an additional seven days. It was enough.

21. After the author has responded, I send the edited manuscript back to the publishing house. A few weeks later (and I never know when it's coming) I receive a second edited version. This is after the copy editor (sometimes called line editor) has gone over the manuscript. She suggests tightening sentences or perhaps moving a paragraph to the next page. I can usually handle all that, but I wait until the author has sent me any of his changes. I incorporate his preferences. Sometimes I send my responses and then ask, "If you're not agreeable to anything, let me know."

Again, we usually have about a week.

22. Most publishers then send the page proofs—how the book will look in print. Here we can make only minor changes that involve typos or bad breaks. (A bad break, for example, is when the computer repeats a word, leaves out a line, or hyphenates a hyphenated word. *Self-satisfied* might look like *self-sat-* with the rest of the word on the next line.) A week later the page proofs go back.

23. Now the author and I wait for the publication of the book.

Takeaways

- The preliminary contact and an in-person meeting must come first. To prepare for that, I look up the individual on the Internet, if there are any links on her, so I can have more information.
- We meet and talk, and if we like each other, we move forward. If we don't, either of us can say no.
- If I say yes, I ask for resources to make me better prepared.
- At an agreed-on date, we meet again, and I conduct the interviews. I tape everything digitally, download it on Dropbox (or some other site), and send the link to my transcriber.
- After having the digital recording transcribed, I organize the material. For me, the organizing takes at least a week.
- When authors speak, I don't try to censor them or redirect unless they stray badly.
- I go over the material and decide the order that fits best with the type of book.
- I devise a preliminary outline and write one or two sentences to explain each chapter.
- Just before I write the proposal, I ask for a resume, which I rewrite using bullets.
- Occasionally I'll suggest endorsers or marketing opportunities through the author's contacts.
- I write the proposal and include a marketing plan.
- After I complete the book proposal, I send it to the author for him to make changes.

- I send back the corrected proposal to make sure I've gotten everything and give her further opportunity to add or change.
- Once the author is satisfied, I send the proposal to my agent.
- My agent decides on a list of publishing houses that she thinks would be open to the book.
- On rare occasions, my agent goes to a book auction.
- Then comes the waiting period—sometimes two or three months after my agent sends out a proposal.
- Under normal conditions I work on something else while I wait.
- We receive an offer. My agent, the author, and I discuss the terms and won't accept unless we agree.
- We sign the contract.
- I go back to work immediately to finish the book.
- I send the full manuscript to the author for changes—as many times as it takes.
- Months later, we receive an edited version with track changes. I make changes and return the manuscript.
- The publishing house usually gives us a week—which is sometimes a rush.
- After the author has responded, I send the edited manuscript back to the publishing house.
- A few weeks later, I receive a second edited version. This is after the copy editor has gone over the manuscript. Again, we usually have about a week.
- Most publishers then send the page proofs, and we can make only minor changes. A week later, the page proofs go back.
- Now the author and I wait for the publication of the book.

ACKNOWLEDGMENTS

So many have contributed to my work and my success as a ghostwriter/collaborator that it's impossible to name them all. I've mentioned many of them in the book—and I'm thankful for their help.

Deidre Knight, who has been my agent for nearly twenty years, deserves recognition for her encouragement in my many ghostwriting efforts, as does Elaine Spencer.

I also want to thank my faithful virtual office assistant, Twila Belk, and her helper, Gail Smith. Many times Twila covered for me when I was overwhelmed by projects. My thanks also to Wanda Rosenberry, who did minor editing and proofing for this book.

Above all, I'm grateful to God for giving me the talent and the opportunity for a career that has enriched my life.